VINTAGE

MY TRUTH

Narmadashankar Lalshankar Dave, or Kavi Narmad, as he is popularly known, was a Gujarati poet, essayist, lexicographer and social reformer. A prolific writer, he had written ten volumes of poetry, and published three edited volumes of his essays and a comprehensive dictionary in Gujarati by the time of his death at the age of fifty-six. His autobiography, *Mari Hakikat*, is the first autobiography ever written in Gujarati.

Abhijit Kothari combines sociology, business and management in his research and teaching. He lives in Ahmedabad, where he runs his own business. He is also the co-translator of K.M. Munshi's iconic Patan trilogy with Rita Kothari.

ADVANCE PRAISE FOR THE BOOK

'Narmad's pioneering autobiography paved the way for modern Gujarat's search for self that gave the language and its people M.K. Gandhi's *My Experiments with Truth*. Narmad's autobiography, ably translated by Abhijit Kothari, greatly enhances the resources through which we understand the making of modern Gujarat's self-sense' —**Tridip Suhrud, provost, CEPT University**

'Narmad's account of himself is a marvellous living portrait of mid-nineteenth-century upper-caste life in western India. Its translation is much to be celebrated and will place an important account of this period in the hands of those who cannot read Gujarati. It is an impressive addition, documenting the financial struggles, family relations, youthful students and the relations of patronage, but also leisure and pleasure. Abhijit Kothari has chosen the autobiography from Narmad's extensive oeuvre. He stays close to Narmad's spoken Gujarati style, demonstrating his youth, his truculence, his loves and hates. This small but poignant autobiography shines a personal, intimate light on the familiar "big events" like the Maharaj Libel Case, the share mania, the cotton boom due to the American Civil War, the reclamation of the Back Bay, the Great Fire of Surat and widow remarriage among others' —**Amrita Shodhan, senior teaching fellow, Department of History, Religions and Philosophies, SOAS, University of London**

My Truth

Autobiography of
Narmadashankar Dave

*Translated from
the Gujarati by*

Abhijit
Kothari

VINTAGE
An imprint of Penguin Random House

VINTAGE

Vintage is an imprint of the Penguin Random House group of companies
whose addresses can be found at global.penguinrandomhouse.com

Published by Penguin Random House India Pvt. Ltd
4th Floor, Capital Tower 1, MG Road,
Gurugram 122 002, Haryana, India

Penguin
Random House
India

First published in Vintage by Penguin Random House India 2025

ISBN 9780143467014

Typeset in Adobe Caslon Pro by MAP Systems, Bengaluru, India
Printed at Gopsons Papers Pvt. Ltd., Noida

www.penguin.co.in

100%
Paper from well-
managed forests
FSC® C191020

About the Chronicles Series

The Ashoka Centre for Translation, through its initiatives, is committed to thinking about translation from a many-to-many perspective to foster India's multilingual ethos. Chronicles is a groundbreaking non-fiction translation series aimed at bringing creative–critical textual narratives from various Indian languages into English. In the inaugural list supported by the Manju Deshbandhu Gupta Fellowship, ten books are being published in partnership with Penguin Random House India.

translation.ashoka.edu.in

Contents

Introduction   ix

Viram 1: Aims   1
Viram 2: Samvat 1811   21
Viram 3: 1833–45   39
Viram 4: 1845–51   52
Viram 5: 1851–54   70
Viram 6: 1854–56   82
Viram 7: 1857–59   102
Viram 8: 1860   141
Viram 9: 1861–64   154
Viram 10: 1865–66   177

Introduction

Ask any ordinary Gujarati today what the name Narmad means to them and they will say that he wrote the poem 'Jay Jay Garvi Gujarat' (Hail to Thee, Glorious Gujarat). It is arguably the first work in which Gujarat has been defined both geographically and culturally. For those slightly more familiar with his life, Narmad is known both as a literary figure and as a social reformer.

Narmadashankar Lalshankar Dave, or Kavi Narmad, was born in Surat on 24 August 1833 in a Nagar Brahmin family. He spent his childhood shuttling between Surat and Bombay. He studied for some time at the Elphinstone Institution, but quit his studies for various reasons. After working as a teacher for a while, he finally decided to devote his life to writing poetry. As he notes in his autobiography, from 23 November 1858 onwards, he decided to make his living exclusively from his writings. He engaged actively with the social reform movement through his writing as well as by his actions. He was a poet, essayist, literary critic, lexicographer, historian and reformer. He (along with Dalpatram, his contemporary) is ranked by almost all critics among the pioneering modern writers in Gujarati. K.M. Munshi's 1939 essay on Narmad is titled 'Narmad: Arvāchinomān Ādya' (Narmad: The First among the Moderns). Sitanshu Yashashchandra, too, credits him as a pioneer of Gujarati prose:

> The major literary and cultural innovations and events of the two decades from 1851 include the first Gujarati essay, 'Mandali Malvathi thata Labh' (The Advantages of Forming Forums [for social reforms]) in 1851 by the pioneer of Gujarati prose, Narmadashankar Lalshankar Dave. (Yashashchandra, 2003, p. 595)

A prolific writer, Narmad, in the period between 1858 and 1866, published ten volumes of his poetry, two volumes of compilations of essays, four books on poetics, three compilations of literary criticism and four volumes of his dictionary. Apart from the sheer volume of production, what is impressive is the range of subjects that he wrote on. *Māri Hakikat*, which documents the first thirty-three years of his life, is the first autobiography in Gujarati and is considered somewhat of a literary landmark.

He is credited with introducing new ideas and subjects, such as romance, nature, travel and social reform, in his poetry. He is also known for his essays, a relatively new literary form which he took to with great panache. As K.M. Munshi notes in his *Gujarat and Its Literature*:

> His essays, inspired by a vivid imagination and written in a rhetorical style, laid the foundation of modern prose literature. (Munshi, 1935, p. 241)

He was an active participant in the social reform movement. The issues that he was primarily concerned with were superstitions, women's education, rigid enforcement of caste rules, widow remarriage and restrictions on travelling abroad. The subjects of some of his essays—'Kelavni Vishe' (On Education), 'Stree Na Dharma' (The Duty of Women), 'Lagna Tatha Punarlagna' (Marriage and Remarriage)—and poems—'Hinduoni Padti' (The Decline of the Hindus), 'Vaidhvyachitra' (A Picture of Widowhood), 'Stree Shikshan Sambandhi' (On Women's Education)—clearly indicate his deep engagement with ideas of social reform. As Dhirubhai Thaker observes in his preface to the critical edition of the autobiography:

> To create literature is one thing; to create new forms of literature is another thing; to create new forms of

literature while participating in social and religious reforms is yet another thing altogether. Narmad was a litterateur who belonged to this third category. (Thaker, 2008, p. vii)

A Historical Context

The nineteenth century in western India saw two important developments brought about by the colonial influence. The British administration in the Bombay Presidency introduced, in the early part of the nineteenth century, a new system of education. By about the 1850s, this led to the implementation of a system wherein education was provided in the vernacular for the early part of primary education. From the fourth year onwards, all subsequent education was in English only. Several vernacular schools were established in the districts of Gujarat. Government English schools were also established in select urban centres under the Presidency, such as in Bombay, Surat, Kheda and Ahmedabad.

For education in the vernacular, there was a need for textbooks and primers. The colonial administrators undertook the task of preparing these. The Bombay Native Schoolbook and School Society was established in 1822 (it was subsequently renamed the Bombay Native Education

Society in 1828). The society's task was to produce books aimed at school children. Colonel George Jervis headed the Native Schoolbook and School Committee and was in charge of getting books translated into Gujarati and published (in this autobiography, Narmad relates how his father, Lalshankar, was employed by Jervis to scribe these translations in order to have them published.) In a short span of four years, starting from 1825, several texts, particularly those on mathematics, science and geography, were translated into Gujarati (Sagar, 2022).

The second important development that took place simultaneously was the development of vernacular printing technology and the establishment of privately run printing presses. The administration, whose presses could not cope with the demand for textbooks, began to contract out printing to these private presses. In Bombay, the Parsis played a pioneering role in this and dominated the publishing scene in Gujarati. By the middle of the nineteenth century, several presses had emerged in urban areas of Gujarat and Ahmedabad, in particular, came to be the most important centre for Gujarati publishing, next only to Bombay. The availability of printing in Gujarati resulted in a proliferation of newspapers, periodicals, magazines and, later, even books. The first Gujarati newspaper, *Bombay Samachar*, was started in 1822. Various other newspapers were established in the decades following 1825, among them *Jam-e-Jamshed* and the *Rast Goftar* in 1854. The first Gujarati magazine, *Vidya Sagar*, was published by Nowrozjee Furdoonjee in 1840. Among the other magazines established during this period were *Buddhhiprakash* in 1851, by the Gujarat Vernacular Society in Ahmedabad, *Gyan Prasarak* (1849), *Jagat Mitra* (1850) and the women's magazine *Streebodh* (1857). As Ellen McDonald notes:

> The period from 1857 to 1865 marks a pivotal point in the development of both the vernacular literature and vernacular printing industry, for both in this period became subsidized products of the educational system. (McDonald, 1968, p. 600)

This proliferation of newspapers, periodicals and magazines had two outcomes. One the one hand, it encouraged all types of writing in Gujarati, including several new genres of writing such as essays, travelogues, biographies, literary criticism and debates. Secondly, it created a whole new class of readers, Gujarati elites who, although familiar with the English language, wanted to read in Gujarati. As R. Isaka observes:

Interestingly, although the Indian elite of this period thus acquired a good knowledge of English, they also began to develop a great interest in their vernacular languages, largely influenced by Western notions of national language and literature. (Isaka, 2004, p. 28)

Many of these elites were wealthy Gujarati and Parsi merchants and professionals who provided the financial support required for the publishing and circulation of Gujarati literary works. They read and supported new writing. Functions were organized at their homes where poets and writers were invited to read out their works and were often rewarded financially. They supported societies and forums where such works were read and discussed. Some of these societies even raised funds to support various poets and writers. This role of merchants and elites in western India as patrons of the arts has been documented with reference to Hindustani classical music (Pradhan, 2001; Niranjana, 2015). It would seem that they played a similar role for Gujarati literature too.

The nineteenth century was also a period of social reform in India. It is beyond the scope of this introduction to provide an exhaustive account of the reform movement across India, but its impact in Maharashtra and Gujarat is clear from the fact that various institutions, societies and fora were established at that time, where intellectuals and young men (and they were mostly men), as a result of their education and exposure to Western thought, questioned many social practices and challenged them publicly. Narmad was no exception. From his role in establishing the Buddhivardhak Sabha to his role in taking on the Vaishnav Maharajs through his poetry, essays and, in many instances, through direct action, Narmad earned a prominent place among the major social reformers of his time. For Narmad, reform meant not only abandoning various ills that held Hindu society 'in a noose', it meant transcending caste identity and embracing a larger identity. Tridip Suhrud, with his customary incisiveness, puts it well:

> Reform entailed rethinking basic norms around which a society was constituted and life was lived. This aspiration was that all people would rise above their particular conditions and contribute towards a common good. Narmad was keenly aware that in order to do so people must feel, and feel passionately, about identities that were broader than what caste could provide. These identities could either be a linguistic–cultural unit like Gujarat or an abstract notion like country. (Suhrud, 2009, p. 23)

Interestingly, later in his life, Narmad changed his radical views on reform and advocated that society should adopt practices that were grounded in its past. He felt that blind adoption of ideas from the West that were alien to a society's past would be impossible to implement, and that ultimately, any society should follow its traditional values, making some allowances for changing times (for a detailed account, see Suhrud, 2009).

The Autobiography

As far as the title is concerned, I have chosen to translate the word '*hakikat*' into 'truth'. The title stays with the idea of truth as an all-encompassing pursuit which may in its service use 'facts' or 'accounts'. That said, local contexts in the autobiography warrant multiple meanings of 'hakikat', and I have provided words such as 'account', 'facts' and 'story' to retain the polyvalence of the word.

In the prefatory note, Narmad states that he is '. . . writing these facts (hakikat) not for others, but for myself. Not for recognition (which I already possess), nor for wealth or position, but to draw upon the past as inspiration for the future.' He qualifies that his autobiography should be treated as a draft since '. . . it is possible that some things that I have stated here may, in the future, prove to be incorrect'.

As mentioned earlier, Narmad's *Mari Hakikat* is the first autobiography in Gujarati. For that reason alone, it is a valuable document. The incipient form of the autobiography is borne out by the way in which it is written. Narmad writes in a form that is a mix of narrative essay and jottings from a diary. He numbers various paragraphs or sections in each chapter. At times, this numbering does not seem to follow any logic. He provides copious footnotes. The chapters themselves he calls '*viram*'—a halt or a place of rest—perhaps signifying various locations in his life's journey that he thought were significant.

The value of this work as a historical document, a chronicle of the times, as it were, is immense. Apart from providing the names of various personalities (both major and minor) who played an important role in social reform, it provides an insight into the way literature was consumed by the elite of that time. It is a document that provides information (even if not detailed) about the education system, the culture of printing and propagation of the printed word and the cultural ecosystem of Bombay in the mid-nineteenth century. It also documents Narmad's own role in certain historical events, such as the famous Maharaj Libel Case.

In the autobiography, Narmad comes across as passionate, ambitious, reflective, impatient, given to bouts of melancholia and depression, and brutally honest about his own failings. He is scrupulous with details, providing detailed accounts of even his expenses and earnings. He has taken pains, as he himself narrates, to refer to almanacs so that he can reconcile dates of the Gregorian calendar with those of the Vikram Samvat. At many places, he provides both dates.

Although, by his own admission, he had never bothered with poetry in his youth, once he decides to devote his life to writing, he proceeds with single-minded determination to understand the rules of prosody, both in Sanskrit and in Hindustani. He reads extensively, writes to various persons for material on prosody and even travels wherever he has to in search of relevant material. This shows his commitment and uncompromising nature. Such is the proficiency he acquires that he finally goes on to write *Pingalpravesh*, one of the early works in Gujarati on prosody and poetics.

He shows the same commitment when it comes to matters of social reform. Not caring for the opprobrium he may garner from society, he acts in accordance with his convictions. He defies the demeaning practice of Bhikshuk women removing their upper garments at community meals by encouraging the women of his own family to break this tradition. He risks being mobbed when he engages in a public debate with Jadunathji, the Vaishnav Maharaj. Despite knowing that his father would face pressure from the community, he refuses to change his stand regarding reform.

When it comes to himself, Narmad does not shy away from narrating his weaknesses. Although he was a radical reformer at the time he wrote this autobiography, he honestly narrates how superstitious he was as a child and as an adolescent. He writes about the period of his life during which he whiled away his time with his companions, consuming intoxicants and womanizing. He is restrained only when writing about events that could affect others, especially his romantic affairs, although he clearly hints at them at several places in the autobiography.

Narmad did not publish the autobiography in his own lifetime. As he himself records, he printed about 400 copies of the book, not for circulation but as a document. As per his wish, the autobiography was published after his death (Suhrud, p. 11).

Abhijit Kothari

References

- A. Pradhan, 'Changing facets of Indian music in a colonial situation: a case study of Bombay 1818-1947' (PhD thesis, University of Bombay, 2001).

- Dhirubhai Thaker, Preface of *Kavi Narmadashankar Lalshankar krut Mari Hakikat ane anya atmakathanatmak lakhano* (Ahmedabad: Gurjar Sahitya Prakashan, 2008).

- Ellen E. McDonald, 'The Modernizing of Communication: Vernacular Publishing in Nineteenth Century Maharashtra', Asian Survey , July 1968, vol. 8, no. 7, *Modernization in South Asian Studies: Essays in a Changing Field* (University of California Press, July 1968), pp. 589-606.

- K.M. Munshi, *Gujarat and its Literature* (Bombay: Longmans Green, 1935).

- R. Isaka, 'Language and Education in Colonial and Post-Colonial India', in T. Sasaki, ed., *Nature and Human Communities* (Tokyo: Springer, 2004).

- S. Sagar, 'Science Texts translated from English into Gujarati: A Translation History', *Translation Today*, vol. 16 (2), 75-102 (2002), DOI: 10.46623/ tt/2022.16.2.ar4

- S. Yashashchandra, 'From Hemchandra to Hind Svaraj: Region and Power in Gujarati Literary

Culture' in Pollock, S., ed., *Literary Cultures in History: Reconstructions from South Asia* (Berkeley: University of California Press, 2003).

- T. Niranjana, 'Performing Modernity Musicophilia in Bombay/Bombay' (TISS working paper no. 2, Tata Institute of Social Sciences, Bombay, January 2015).
- T. Suhrud, *Writing Life Three Gujarati Thinkers* (New Delhi: Orient BlackSwan, 2009).

Viram 1

Aims

That someone like me should write his own account and then publish it during his lifetime may seem inappropriate to others—I am neither pandit, nor warrior, nor religious leader, nor dhoti-clad merchant-prince. Many feel that I am, in my writing, rather vainglorious, and they are justified in feeling so. When they do not understand the essence of my writing and mock me or criticize me without considering the tireless effort that I put into my writing, it angers me no end, and this anger seeps through. Perhaps they will call me boastful; let them—at least they will try to understand me. It is not uncommon for others, in their preface, to present their efforts and to speak of themselves— albeit behind a curtain of modesty.

I am writing these facts not for others, but for myself. Not for recognition (which I already possess), nor for wealth or position, but to draw upon the past as inspiration for the future.

Some say that the truth may be written but should not be published. I see a greater benefit in keeping printed papers rather than written papers. With written papers, one needs to make sure that one doesn't misplace them. One is also tempted to go back and revise what one has written time and again if it is unpublished. I have, till date, not waited to publish a volume of work after completing it in its entirety. I publish as I write. I enjoy writing new material. I am loath to go back and revise it. It is also difficult to find a good copy editor. So what I write is a draft and what I publish may be considered the edited version.

The reasons for writing this narrative are as follows: 1) It is not a practice to write about oneself. I want to start this practice. 2) Dr Bhau Daji, Bhai Karsandas Mulji, Bhai Rustamji Gustadji (Irani) in particular and many others have often expressed a desire to know these facts and have said 'give us the story of your life'. 3) I too will realize what is right and what is wrong. 4) Many facts are not available after death—already, when I am barely thirty-three, there are many contradictory facts about me circulating among my relatives. What will happen after my death? As an example, I had asked those from my maternal side if I was born late at night or early in the morning (I have lost my horoscope). They said that it was after sunrise. Those on my father's side, on the other hand, said it was at night. Now what is the truth? After some thought, I have concluded that those on my mother's side were correct. A woman goes to her maternal home for the birth of her child. Since my father's side was informed of my birth in the morning, they must have assumed that I was born the previous night. Take another example. I had asked my old *masi* (my mother's sister) if my mother went to Bombay before my birth or after. She said after. On my father's side, they said it was before my birth. When I asked my *masi* again, she said, 'Bhai, nowadays even the newlyweds have begun to go to Bombay. Earlier, Bombay had a bad reputation (this is true) and the parents of a new bride were reluctant to send their daughters there. Husbands who were older were also reluctant to take their new brides there. Your mother went to Bombay for the first time, taking you along, when you were only about ten months old. This much is certain.' 5) It has taken me six months to reconcile the dates of the Gregorian and the Vikram Samvat calendars after locating old almanacs going back thirty-two years. Who else, assuming that they wanted to know the facts of my life, would be willing to do this after my death?

For these reasons, I am publishing in note form these facts in brief. Some events are already described in my other prose and poetry publications. I am not repeating those here.

This story is incomplete and should be treated as a draft. It is incomplete because I do not think it appropriate to narrate certain events that would cause pain to some relatives and others who have been associated with me (I do not show such consideration towards myself). It is a draft because due to my incomplete knowledge and in my haste to publish (I publish as I write), it is possible that some things that I have stated here may, in the future, prove to be incorrect.

With all this, I will not write here what I do not consider proper to put down; but what I do write will be correct to the best of my knowledge, whether it presents me in a good light or bad, whether others approve or not.

In 1854, I had begun making notes about my life, but not on a regular basis. I had not thought at the time that I would write an account of my life. Had that been so, I would have maintained a regular diary. But those notes, my father's words and those of my friends, relatives and fellow caste members, as well as some records of expenses found from my house, have better equipped me to write this account of my life.

1.   I was conceived in my ancestral home in the Aamliraan
     *mohalla** of Surat and was born in my mother's maternal
     home located in Kotwali Sheri in the early morning
     hours of Bhadarva Sud 10 of Samvat 1889 or 24
     August 1833. My horoscope is lost, and I do not have it
     any more. My father was not in Surat at the time of my
     birth. Since I was born during the Jyeshta Nakshatra,
     which is considered inauspicious, we had to conduct

---

* It was named Amliraan because, before the great fire, there were
five huge imli trees at a distance of about five–six yards from one
another. The girth of each tree was so large that it would take two
men to embrace it. The canopies loomed over the roof of our house.
The homes of our ancestors were located under these trees. The path
between these trees and our home was perpetually in the shade of the
canopy and after sunset, it was dark enough to be as fearsome as a
forest. Few outsiders would venture here after dark, fearing thieves and
the ghosts said to haunt the imli trees. These trees and our homes were
engulfed by the great fire that broke out in the early morning of Chaitra
Vad 5 of Samvat 1893 or Tuesday, 25 April 1837. In Samvat 1894, my
father and uncles began building new homes with four divisions, which
were finally completed towards the end of Samvat 1895. While coming
from the entrance of the mohalla, the first two divisions of the house
belong to the children of my uncle and the next two are mine. There
was a charred open ground in front of my house, which I bought this
January for Rs. 600, to build on. This land originally lay between the
two imlis—and I bought it for its symbolic value.

the Jyeshta Shanti puja to eradicate the ill effects of this astrological configuration. My father could see my face in Samvat 1890 only after he paid Rs. 100 to conduct this puja once he arrived from Bombay.

2. We are said to be from the Aukshnas *gotra*. All Brahmins are said to have descended from eight rishis—Gautam, Atri, Bharadwaj, Kashyap, Vashisht and Vishwamitra. These are the eight primary gotras, and all Brahmins trace their origins to one of these rishis, which is then considered their gotra. So there are only eight primary gotras. But according to the authors of several texts, the first forty-nine descendants of these eight can also be considered gotras. Some others say that each of the descendants (up to the second generation) of the eight rishis can be considered to form his own separate gotra. Among these descendants, whether the first generation or the second, there was a rishi named Aukshnas, and he is considered the founder of our gotra, the one to whom we trace our lineage. I was curious to trace the period of this Aukshnas and I asked a shastri if these gotras were to be traced to the beginning of the current Kaliyug or the beginning of the Satyug of the current cycle. After all, there must have been several such

cycles of Satyug and Kaliyug. The shastri replied that there was no clear answer, but the eight original rishis were said to have existed during the early part of the Shvet Varaha Kalpa. Since there must have been many persons named Vashisht and many named Aukshnas, I then asked him how we would know which of them was our primary ancestor (I did not get any response).

Our gotra has three *pravaras*. This means that the founder of our lineage had employed three *ritvijas* (Brahmins who assisted in conducting rituals) for his sacrificial rituals. These three were named Vashishta, Shakti and Parashar. Earlier, Brahmins became ritvijas for one another; there was no distinction of Grihastha and Bhikshuk as exists today. According to one shastri, the pravara is defined by the rishi who is associated with the *stuti*s uttered during the yajna. Each gotra recites the names of different rishis during the yajna. The *kalpasutra* of their branch specifies these names, and accordingly, each gotra has one, two, three or five pravaras. There is no existence of a gotra having four pravaras. Some others say that the ancestors each gotra chooses to revere define their pravara.

We are Rigvedis—i.e., our original ancestor and his descendants chose to study the Rig Veda. Our *shakha* (branch) is Shankhayani. The Rig Veda is said to have eight branches—the eight original rishis had prescribed distinct ways in which to recite the Vedic mantras and conduct Vedic rituals. Our original ancestor adopted the method of Rishi Shankhayan. Some also believe that the different methods of reciting and teaching the Vedas demarcate the different *shakhas (adhyayan aadhyapan avashaat bhedaah)*.

Traditionally, our forefathers had affixed the title Sharm to identify our family. The word Sharm was added at the end of the name to denote that we are Brahmins. Similarly, the Kshatriyas used Varm, the Vaishyas Gupt and the Shudras Das. The word Sharm merely denoted that the person was born into a Brahmin family. But now there is further distinction in Sharm to denote the specific Brahmin family. The gotra only defined the original rishi or ancestor, and there were many members of a gotra. Hence, the name of any one well-known ancestor within the family was adopted in addition to Sharm. Our ancestors were known as Duttsharm or Sharmsharm, etc., since they were Brahmins. A well-known ancestor of our family was named Sharm, and our surname would hence be Sharm-Sharm (Sharm is a common noun as well as a proper noun), and I should be known as Narmadashankar Sharm-Sharm. But this practice is no longer in vogue (it is used only during specific rituals).

Besides, of late, there has begun a practice of placing Dvivedi or its common form Dave before our name. Our ancestors studied two Vedas—the Rig and the Yajur.

The highest among the *jaati*s was the Brahmin, and among them, those who learnt the Vedas were considered superior to those who only learnt the Shastras (*Vedadhyayi Sadaashivah*). Earlier, those who learnt the Vedas could actually debate and discuss their meaning. This, then, is an account of our distant ancestors.

3. Many years later, our ancestors and some others came to settle in Anandpur or Vadnagar in Gujarat. There, they came to be known as Nagar Brahmins. According to the *Pravaraadhyaya* of the Nagars, it seems that there were 1,500 gotras among the Brahmins of Anandpur. Of these, those that existed before Samvat 283 came to be known as Nagars. Our narrative of the Nagar Brahmins is as follows:

Many, knowingly or unknowingly, accepted gifts/alms from the Shudras and they also migrated to other

locations. Accordingly, the Nagars were subdivided
into six groups—Vadnagara or Talabda Shuddha
Nagar, Visalnagara, Sathodara, Chitroda, Prashnora
and Krushnora. King Visaldev established Visalnagar
(in Samvat 936) and conducted the Kapotvadh Yajna.
Some Nagars went to attend the yajna. When the king
offered them dakshina, the Nagars said that they did
not accept dakshina from anyone. The king, however,
inscribed the names of villages in betel leaves and
offered them to the Nagars. Thus, he cheated them
into accepting dakshina. The Nagars of Vadnagar, on
learning this, cast those that had attended the yajna out
of their Vadnagar Nagar caste group. In this manner,
the six groups came into being.

> On the Reva river is village Sathod, accepting its
> gift deed,
> Leaving Vadnagar, did they adopt the title Sathodara.
> Visaldev the king, generous and religious was he
> To attend his Kapotvadh Yajna, did two braves go
> He tricked them concealing a note in the betel leaf
> He gifted them Visalnagar, unknowingly did
> they accept.
> —etc., etc., etc.

It is said that the Nagars have seventy-two gotras. But Dinmanishankar Shastri has specified sixty-four gotras as follows:

Kaushik, Kashyap, Darbha, Lakshman, Harikar, Vatspaal, Etikaayan, Udvahal, Bharadwaj, Vaarah, Maunaya, Kaundinya, Aalaubhayan, Parashar, Gaupal, Aukshna, Gautam, Baijvaap, Shandilya, Chhandogya, Aatreya, Vriddhaatreya, Krishnadheya, Dattatreya, Kaurangap, Gaalav, Kaapishtal, Jaatukarna, Gauraayat, Shaargav, Gaagyaayan, Sankrutya, Shaarkraaksh, Pippalaad, Shaakayan, Gaargya, Maatkaayan, Paanineya, Laukaaksh, Kaushal, Agniveshya, Haarit, Chandrabhargav, Aangiras, Kautsya, Maandavya, Mauddabh, Jaimineya, Paithinasi, Gaubhil, Kaatyayan, Vasishtha, Naidhruva, Narayan, Jaabaali, Jamdagni, Shalihotra, Nadhush, Agastya, Aushnas, Bhagurayan, Traivaneya, Vaitaayan and Chyavan.

Of these sixty-four, the eight highest gotras are assigned as under:

Kaashyapashchaiva Kaundinya Aukshnashah
Sharkvodvisha

Baijavaapah Shashtamah Prokto
Kapishthoturukstanaha

The eight gems of culture are these—Kashyap, Kaundinya, Aukshna, Sharkav, Kaushik, Baijavpaha, Kapishta and Gautam.

Accordingly, I belong to one of the eight (ah, what vanity!).

4. When Vadnagar was conquered, the Nagars escaped to other locations. Among these were my elders, who came to Surat. It is said that Vadnagar was conquered thrice. The first time was in the Magha month of Samvat 645 by the Muslims, when some Nagars escaped to Patan. The second time was in the month of Kartik of Samvat 1272 by Gorisha (probably Shahbuddin Ghori). At that time, some Nagars escaped and settled in Junagadh and some in Idar and Ahmedabad (Ahmedabad was founded after Samvat 1467–68. I believe that they must have settled in areas around what we today call Ahmedabad). The third time Vadnagar fell was Samvat 1782, under attack from the Marathas, and almost all the Nagars of Vadnagar left and settled in Idar, Vaasvalu, Dungarpur, Kashi and Mathura. I have obtained these details from the sixth *kadva* or section

of an old text, 'The marriage of Narsinh Mehta's son', by one Vallabhdas. On the request of some, I am reproducing the entire sixth kadva here:

The caste took a decision together and all were much relieved

How did Narsinh become Mehta, how did he come to leave Vadnagar

I will relate all at length, O hear me patiently

Many years thus went by, kingdoms were ruled by the Kshatriyas

The Yavanas struck Hastinapur and the Nagars did go there

They served there and reaped the fruits, hear me as I describe it all

Samvat six hundred forty-five, in fear of the Yavanas

The town fell in the month of Magha, let me tell you the story entire

The lord of Patan, a devout man was he

Half the Nagars there did go, all the valiant ones

Eighteen thousand were they, householders twelve thousand

Six thousand single ones, in service of Mahadev

Half went into the town and forever settled there

Those that didn't were called Aabhitar, the settlers
named Adhvaas

In matters of caste and community, of one mind
they were

All gathered together at occasions when invited
they were

The Adhvaas that stayed in Siddhpur Patan,
over time

By practices and rituals, with Vadnagar did not align

Many more years went by, all prospered in kingdoms
respective

Some adopted the Kshatriya way and came to be
Raajanshis

Some others adopted trade, and Grihasthis were
they called

The last group of Brahmins studied the Vedas

Thus it came to pass that three groups were formed

The first time Vadnagar fell was due to the mlechchhas,

The second time happened this way, so says Vallabhdas

Samvat twelve seventy-two, in the month of Kartik

Gorisha was on his way back after the great loot

Navghan the king of Junagadh, three lakh riders hath he

Two thousand fled and sought refuge under him

The townsmen with great respect did the Nagars receive
Were offered posts in the kingdom, their advice well-received
At that same time one thousand to Idar did flee
Five thousand obstinate ones in Vadnagar did stay
In the same manner Amdavadis were called Adhvaasi
The Sorathis, two thousand, Aabhyantar were they called
Twelve towns of the Adhvaasis and twelve of the Sorathis
Of those that stayed in Vadnagar, listen to this tale
(1782) Samvat seventeen eighty-two it was
And the Marathas did rampage
All the Nagars fled the town abandoning all hope
To Idar, Valambh, Vaansvalu, Dungarpur and Patan
To Kashi and Mathura to save their lives did they flee
Thus did the town fall in this Kali Age
From Vadnagar did six towns emerge
And sub-groups further three
With the grace of Lord Shiva, all gained prosperity
Those that left the Vedas did meet with poverty
For when the Veda and rituals they gave up, Shiva dimmed their light
Now let me go on and tell you Narsinh Mehta's plight

From the above it can be seen that three distinct groups were formed—Nagar Brahmins, Nagar Grihastha (those in trade and government service) and Nagar Kshatriya (kings and soldiers or Sipahi Nagars).

5. No one seems to have written on when and how the Nagars arrived in Surat. Some old Nagar Brahmins of Surat say, 'We first escaped to Champaner and thence further to Surat and areas around it.' Even today, the Nagars of Surat distinguish themselves as Adajania, Navsarigara, Valsadiya, Baranporia, etc. Champaner* fell on Pausha Sud 3 of Samvat 1540 and the establishment of Surat occurred around approximately Samvat 1570 and onwards. So it does seem as if the Brahmins came to settle in areas where the Hindus were in power to escape harassment at the

---

* The last king of Champaner was Raval Jesing, aka Patai. It is likely that the Brahmins stayed in Champaner as long as it was ruled by Hindu kings and fled upon the arrival of Muslim rulers. The *Rasmala* mentions that the Rao of Idar bore a grudge against the Raval of Champaner. The Rao, taking the help of the Muslims, attacked Champaner and although the Raval of Champaner was supported by the Sultan of Malwa, he lost and Champaner was taken over by Mohammed Begda of Ahmedabad on 27 November 1484 CE.

hands of the Muslims. Further, the Brahmins of Surat say that the first Brahmins stayed in Fulpada village for about seventy-five years, and then came to the city of Surat. It has been 150 years since they came to the city. The third migration from Vadnagar also occurred 140 years ago. But since Vallabhdas makes no mention of Surat, it is likely that they came to Champaner from Idar. Now, according to Vallabhdas, Idar was the destination during the second migration of the Nagars from Vadnagar. So we belong to the group that escaped during the second migration and either went to Idar from Vadnagar or to Junagadh and then to Idar.* From Idar, we must have moved to Champaner, then gradually spread to various villages along the way and finally settled in Surat.

---

* The Nagars first came to Idar (I believe from Vadnagar) during the reign of Samaliyo Sodh, a Hindu king. From here they spread out to Champaner and beyond. This entire migration occurred over a period of 250 years. The *Rasmala* has to this to say about the Nagars of Idar: One of the descendants of Samaliyo decided to marry the daughter of one of his Nagar administrators. That Nagar invited Sonangji Rathod and destroyed the Sodh dynasty. I believe that soon after this, the Muslim rulers in the area must have harassed the Nagars and they must have come to settle in Champaner.

6. Gujarat has no Sipahi Nagars (they are found towards
    Kashi and Gwalior). Vallabhdas has described two
    events that led to the formation of the Grihastha and
    the Bhikshuk groups. The second instance is in the
    poem cited earlier. The first instance is that some had
    to take up arms in the cause of protecting the Vedic
    religion. They came to be known as Grihastha. Those
    who continued with conducting sacrificial rites and
    rituals came to be known as Bhikshuks. They could
    accept dakshina from each other as well as from the
    Grihasthas. The Grihastha will not accept dakshina
    from a Bhikshuk. Originally, these Brahmins would
    not accept dakshina from Vaniyas etc., but nowadays
    they accept from everyone. In fact, some Brahmins
    even conduct rituals for the Vaniyas. This group is
    known as Dhankada in Surat. Those that remain true
    to their path are known as Kunkanas. If a Kunkana
    gives a girl in marriage to a Dhankada (this happens
    only rarely), he has to pay a fine. Unlike the Bhikshuk
    group, the Grihasthas do not have Pandyas and Daves
    among them since they no longer study the Vedas.

7. Nowadays, the youth among the Grihasthas consider
    Bhikshuks to be lower than them. But if one considers

the duty of their lineage, it is they who abandoned it and are hence lower. Of course, if one considers wealth and material status, the Grihasthas are certainly higher. But that is not of concern to me. The elders still venerate the Bhikshuks. Nowadays, the Brahmins do not rely so much on the Grihasthas; they have adopted newer occupations in keeping with the times. Under these circumstances, it does not behove the wise Nagars to maintain the distinctions of Grihastha and Bhikshuks, to restrict marriages among them and to keep alive other such divisive practices. I may be considered a Bhikshuk Nagar by birth, but where have I practised any of the Bhikshuk's duties? I have been brought up in the best traditions of a Grihastha. I firmly believe that the Grihasthas must give up their sense of superiority and the Bhikshuks must give up their rights/claims of being a Bhikshuk along with all undesirable practices. Marriages between the two must be allowed without any restrictions. These reforms should not be restricted to any particular city, but must be propagated among all Nagars so that their plight and position may improve. Among the people of Gujarat, the Nagars have been considered to occupy the highest position in terms of social status, appearance, knowledge and wisdom, and continue to be regarded as such (I will elaborate on this issue some other time).

The above lengthy narration is as such irrelevant as far as I am concerned and therefore should not have been written. But there are many among the Brahmins of Gujarat who have no idea as to what gotra or pravara is. It is for their sake and for the sake of my fellow Nagars, with whom I would like to share the history of the Nagars (obtained with great effort by me), that I have written the above—certainly not to boast about me or about my being a Nagar.

Viram 2

Samvat 1811

My great-grandfather, Narayan Dave, had studied the Vedas and achieved great proficiency through the study of the Panchkavyas, the five canonical works of Sanskrit poetry. He had learnt the Mantrashastras and was well-versed in performing the Vedic rituals. He was an Agnihotri. Dinmanishankar Shastri, the elders of my community as well as my father say that Narayan Dave had acquired certain supernatural powers. Once, he arranged a feast for the community to celebrate his son's marriage. Sweets were prepared for about 300 people. In the room where the sweets were stored, a ghee lamp was lit and was kept constantly burning. He himself would fetch the sweets from the room and give them to the servers. He had issued instructions to the members of the family that they should not look at the lamp. From the sweets prepared for 300 persons, he fed three times as many people. The people present were astonished. A few of them instigated his wife into opening the locked storeroom. As soon as she entered and looked inside, the lamp went out and everything went dark. No one could see anything. Ordinarily, Narayan Dave eked out a living through the grace of his *jajmans*.

He had three sons—Purushottam, Vishwottam and Narottam. Vishwottam was married but did not have any children. Narottam had two children—a son, Kikabhai, and a daughter, Shivgauri, but they died young and his lineage was also extinguished. And as for the elder Purushottam, my father's father, I will narrate as under.

My grandfather—my father's father—Purushottam Dave, had studied the *dasha granth*s. The *dasha granths* are all the Samhitas, Pada, Kram, the six Angas (Shiksha, Sutra, Ashtadhyayi, Nirukta, Chhand and Jyotish) and the Brahmanas. He had also read three commentaries on the *Kaumudi*, a Sanskrit grammar text, as well as the Panchkavyas, so his proficiency in the language was excellent. He had not mastered any specific shastra, but he would read the Bhagvadpurana and other Puranas in the original. He had a good understanding of poetics and prosody but did not write poetry. His knowledge of prosody can be deduced from the fact that he had studied the Chhand Anga and knew his Sanskrit. Besides, Bhadrashankar Dikshit, who was recognized for his mastery over Sanskrit poetics and prosody, was his close friend. His calligraphy in the Balbodh script was exceptional. Many of his handwritten books are said to be read even today.

He earned his living conducting Vedic rituals for others, as a scribe, and through his reading of the Puranas. He owned residential property worth Rs 3,000, from which his annual rental income was about Rs 100. Thus, his total annual income from all sources was about Rs 300.

His wife, Gaurivahu (maiden name Dhankunvar), bore his first child, a boy named Jaishankar, but he died at the age of five. Many years later, she bore him three sons, Ichchhashankar, Venishankar and my father, in that order. Ichchhashankar was born in Samvat 1856 and died on Bhadarva Vad 5 of 1910. Venishankar was born in 1859 and died in 1892. I know virtually nothing about Venishankar except that he married twice but had no children. Ichchhashankar *kaka* was gentle and affectionate, and was adept at worldly dealings within the community. He had read the entire Rig Veda Samhita, but he served as a *talati* with the government. He is survived today by his widow, two sons and a daughter.

To manage the sacred thread ceremony of his three sons, Purushottam Dave conducted readings of the Vedas as well as the Puranas in Bombay, Bhavnagar and Vadodara. In this manner, he managed to earn Rs 1000. His nature was such that he would travel out of home only when he needed the money. The rest of the time he spent at home, occupied in his study of the Vedas and making copies of others' books (he could write seventy-five shlokas in good handwriting in two hours). There were an unestimated number of books in the home, but they were all burnt down in the Great Fire. For the marriage of his three sons, he needed Rs 6,000. He borrowed this sum from Amritram (aka Bhanjabhai), the son of his sister-in-law's daughter, who was a wealthy man.

Purushottam was fair and short-statured. He did not have much wealth by way of jewellery or money, but there was a large amount of grain stored in the house. He took great pains to educate his children. He was quiet by temperament, loved his family, was contented and, although not rich, was extremely principled. He would go to read the Vedas and Puranas only if invited by others. He never sought such opportunities through flattery or appeasement. An example of his principled stand is an incident when, on his way back from the Balaji temple, he decided to pay a visit to Travadi, a rich merchant. Someone instigated Travadi to jokingly ask, 'So, Daveji, have you come to inveigle an invitation?' Daveji simply replied in the affirmative and left. Since that day, not only did he never visit Travadi again, he also stopped going to the Balaji temple. Travadi sent him invitations on several occasions when rituals were to be conducted, but Daveji declined them all. He always worshipped an earthen image of Shiva. Purushottam Dave left his earthly body at the age of sixty-two on Kartik Vad 6 of Samvat 1884.

Not much is known about his wife, my father's mother, Dhankunvar or Gaurivahu. It is known that her father, Ganpat Dikshit, enjoyed the patronage of Sagram Vasi, the father of Hari Vasi Desai. Hence, he was able to help his sister's family in times of need. My grandmother died four to five years after my grandfather in Samvat 1888 at the age of fifty-five. She was a gentle, content and loving soul.

My maternal grandfather, Ochhavram, earned his living as a Brahmin. His gotra was Baijavaap. He died in Samvat 1883–84 at the age of about sixty. He sang well. His brother Dullabhram, who used to accompany my mother and me on our trips to Bombay and back, had a lot of affection for us. Oh, such sweet memories I have of sitting with him as a child on the veranda, listening to his tales and being fascinated by his wrinkled skin! My mother's mother, Ichchhalakhmi, was a meek and loving person.

My father, Lalshankar, was born on Posh Sud 9 of Samvat 1864. As a child, he was quite short, fair, quick yet quiet. He got his *upavita sanskar*, sacred thread, at the age of five. He studied till he was seventeen—two major sections of the Rig Veda Samhita, three commentaries of Sarasvat, four chapters of *Raguvamsha*, one chapter of *Kumarsambhava* and the *Kaumudi* up to the Stree Pratyaya. He learnt how to write from his father, who was also a scribe. At the age of eighteen, he started sitting at the town square, writing documents for people. At the age of nineteen, on Maha Sud 5 of Samvat 1883, he got married, and shortly after the wedding in the month of Vaishakh, he got a job in Bombay. It so happened that the government was undertaking the printing of textbooks for schools, and the work was assigned to Captain (later Colonel) Jervis. In those days, unlike today, typesetting was not known; books were printed using the litho-press technology and good calligraphers were required for this. The Maharashtrian scribes could not understand the Gujarati script or write it. Jervis wrote to Mr. Jones, the judge of the Surat court, to send him some good scribes. Jones conducted a test for the scribes in the court. Lalshankar was sent to appear for this test at the instance of Bhanjabhai, his nephew (who had a soft corner for our family and had done us many favours). The scribes in those days used thick letters, but Lalshankar's calligraphy, from the very beginning, had fine, clear letters. He was among the ten candidates selected by Jones and asked to proceed to Bombay at a salary of Rs 30. My grandfather was bedridden at the time and my grandmother did not give him permission to go to Bombay. Bhanjabhai taunted them, saying, 'How will you return the Rs 6,000 that was borrowed for the thread ceremony of the three brothers? So better not turn down this opportunity of a steady job.' This taunt cut Lalshankar to the quick, and he immediately proceeded to Bombay. He worked there for a year at a salary of Rs 30 and for one more year at a salary of Rs 45. But then the government moved the printing press to Pune. Jervis was willing to offer a salary of Rs 60 if Lalshankar moved to Pune, but his mother refused and therefore he declined. Jervis gave him a certificate and Rs 135. The certificate says, 'Lalshankar writes Gujarati and Balbodh script very beautifully.'

After this, Lalshankar spent three years in Surat. Here, on this piece of land which I have now purchased and where originally Bhanjabhai's house stood, he worked as a scribe from morning to night save for a lunch break. He charged Rs 3 per thousand words and worked enough to make at least one rupee every day. When the government finally shut down its press in Pune, many incomplete books were taken up for printing by other privately owned presses in Bombay. He was once again made an offer, which he accepted, and went to Bombay, where he continued his original work at a salary of Rs 30.

In the meantime, there was a vacancy for the post of a clerk in the Sudder Court in Bombay at a salary of Rs 15. Lalshankar applied and was selected. He joined on 7 January 1835. His salary was increased to Rs 20–25 and in October 1857, further increased to Rs 30.

Age and weakness were catching up with him. Not able to work anymore, Lalshankar retired with a pension of Rs 10 per month on 7 February 1863. In September, he returned to Surat. His weakness increased and he was bedridden. He suffered a stroke and could not speak for four days. On Posh Sud 10 of Samvat 1920 or 18 January 1864, he left this world one day after his fifty-sixth birthday.

I have not seen any Gujarati as industrious as Lalshankar. He rose daily at 4 a.m. He would work on scribing for the printing presses till 9. In the meantime, my mother would have finished her cooking. He would have his lunch and leave at ten sharp for the court. He would walk the

1.5-mile distance to the court. He would work at the court till 6 p.m. On his way back, he would purchase provisions for home. At home, he would once again work at scribing for the newspapers till 8.30, have his dinner and after a brief respite, would continue with his scribing work till 11–12 in the night. Although scribing for newspapers required great care, he had the ability to swiftly continue his work, even while carrying on a conversation with any visitor or my mother and myself. He charged one rupee for four large pages in the Balbodh script or one rupee for six pages in Gujarati. There are many books written in his hand. It is probable that no other scribe has written as much as he did. A significant number of the books printed in the few litho presses of Bombay at the time were transcribed by him. There are a large number of books scribed by him in Balbodh that were printed in Jervis's press. In addition, there are several other works—the *Bhagwat*, *Chandipaath* etc.—that he scribed but that were never published.

He was the first to copy the chapter on trigonometry in the textbook *Shikshamala Book 2*. Some of the best examples of his Balbodh script are the books *Vidya Uddesh Labh Ne Santosh* in Gujarati and *D'Morgan's Algebra* in Marathi. In the Gujarati script, notable examples are *Bhugolvidya* (in small letters), the first edition of *Sansar Chopadi* and the

essay 'Mandali Malvathi Thata Laabh'. The first edition
of *Pingalpravesh* and *Rasapravesh* were also examples of
his craft. In an effort to preserve his beautiful Balbodh
lettering, I had had the *Chandipaath* written by him on
gold-coloured paper, which he wrote in the most beautiful,
clear calligraphy. When Dr Bhau Daji saw it, he expressed a
desire to keep it in his library, and I gave it to him, much to
my chagrin. Unfortunately, it didn't stay with him since he
took it out to have it bound and someone stole it from him.
Lalshankar used to say, 'In Jervis's department, there was
a Marathi scribe who had no equal in the entire Bombay
presidency. I was next only to him but now, due to age, my
handwriting has deteriorated.'

Despite all this hard work, he did not fail in contributing
to his home. My mother's ill health confined her to bed for
almost two years, and he attended to all the tasks at home.
When he stayed in Surat, the presses would insist that he
send them copies by post from Surat. Writing, writing and
more writing—that seemed to be his life's purpose.

Many would attribute his industriousness to greed.
But no! That wasn't the case. The aim of his effort was
to ensure that we were well taken care of, that he could
discharge his responsibilities towards his friends and kin,
and that he could maintain a good standing within the

caste. There wasn't anything else to rely on and so he had to work this hard. Further, as the saying goes, fortune favours the brave. The press owners were completely enamoured of his handwriting and insisted on giving him assignments. Bapu Harsheth Devlekar paid him the ultimate tribute—after Lalshankar's death, he never published a Gujarati book since it would have meant employing another scribe.

Despite working in the Sudder Court, he never appeared for the lawyer's or *munsif*'s (junior judge's) examination. The reason was that he was focused on immediate benefits. He had no desire to either employ flattery as a lawyer or be subjected to reprimands of superiors as a *munsif*. He said, 'People respect government employees, but these employees have to listen to the reprimands of their colonial bosses and have to resort to sycophancy, which I am aware of. God has given my hands the strength, and so I would rather live without these worries. One often has to compromise with one's principles while occupying higher positions.'

Once Vidyaram, the head clerk, told Lalshankar, 'I want a book to be scribed. So come to my home and write it.' My father replied, 'I will not come to your home. I can write it from my home.' This incident and a previous one, when my father had been rather forthright with him, turned the head clerk against my father, and he made sure that my father didn't get a raise. He couldn't have him fired since my father was an old and experienced hand.

Lalshankar was straightforward in his dealings with others—he delivered his advice in a quiet manner, and his advice was honest, sometimes brutally so. He scrupulously maintained an account of expenses—both his own and that of the household. In social matters, too, he was always practical.

As long as he worked in Jervis's department, he did not work for private clients. On returning from work, he would meet his friends Ranchhoddas Girdharbhai, Khimji Bhat and some Maharashtrians. They would go for a stroll, enjoy themselves by listening to music, *harikatha* etc. Similarly, for the three years that he was in Surat, he did not work nights, preferring to spend time with his friends. But he did not socialize through the day, not even to attend community meals. Such was his regularity at work. From the day he started working at the Sudder court at a salary of Rs 15, he began to work really hard. In 1860, I requested him to stop his work as a scribe, and he finally acceded to my request.

He could understand Sanskrit, even managed to speak it a little bit. Due to his association with the Maharashtrians, he could speak and write in Marathi also. Since he scribed many textbooks, he acquired some knowledge of those subjects, and, of course, his expertise in Gujarati was never a matter of doubt. Ah, the letters he wrote were the epitome of the perfection of language! They were worthy of comparison with those of Pope, Byron or Cowper. It is a pity that I did not preserve them—such simplicity and such purity of language! Even his advice on worldly matters would be interspersed with Sanskrit shlokas! I freely admit that I will never be able to write letters like him. I read a few letters that he wrote to my mother and my mother's responses to him. What love, what standards! And his letters to me—such gentleness, such affection, such wise counsel! Oh, bhai! I miss you so much! I stayed in Surat for three years after the death of my mother. At that time, he was working and living by himself in Bombay. He was copying the book *Madhavaanal* at that time. When he reached the portion when Madhav is exiled and his father weeps, he was overcome with emotion and his quill fell from his hands. I will never forget the vivid description of this episode in his letter to me. He should get some credit for the fame that Samaldas's books have received. It was he who had advised the printer Bapu Harsheth Devlekar to publish them—that it would be to the benefit of the press and the public in general. He had found the handwritten manuscripts in the house of his landlord and had convinced him to part with them for publishing, promising that the landlord would receive one set of the printed copies. Since he himself did not have any knowledge of poetics or prosody, he transcribed them for the press exactly as per the manuscript.

He took great care of books. There were many Sanskrit works in our old house. He had annotated them and had them bound. Unfortunately, they were consumed by a great fire.

He did not have any love for Gujarati poetry but had a good knowledge of music. He enjoyed singing and was himself a good singer. He had started listening to music in his childhood and had heard Vijayanand of Surat. He was also well-acquainted with the singer Bhimanand, Vijayanand's relative. But ever since I started writing poetry, he cultivated his knowledge of poetry and eventually began to read poetry for his own enjoyment. He would say, 'Bhai, your poetry makes me overcome with emotions, so much so that I weep, but it gives me great pleasure nevertheless.'

He was in agreement with the ideas of the social reformers but maintained that 'This is not the right time. As time goes by, things will change.' On caste inequality, he said to me, 'If twenty-five other persons are willing to dissent, you may join them.' Many would criticize me for my thoughts on remarriage. To them, he had this to say, 'Bhai! To each their own. What is wrong in what he says? He has been advising me also to get remarried.' He used to attend the meetings of the Buddhivardhak Sabha, seating himself on the chair opposite whenever I was to deliver an address. He once even read an essay on truth. Despite my active involvement in the social reform movement, he never expressed any disapproval towards me.

His love for me knew no bounds. He always prioritized my needs and never acted against my wishes. He would write out my works for me and I, too, would first read my essays and poems to him. He would recommend making changes only when he felt that I was transgressing certain boundaries, and at such times I complied with his advice. So far, with one exception, I cannot recall any instance of his having taunted or criticized me—he preferred giving gentle advice instead. I am forever regretful that he chose not to marry again. He has tolerated my faults as well as borne the brunt of my misadventures. Yet, he has always offered support and encouragement to me in my endeavours.

By nature, he was affectionate, principled, quiet, contented and yet, capable of enjoyment. He won the affection of all those who came to know him well. He was careful with his expenses but could be lavish when the occasion demanded it. He was respected and enjoyed a high stature in the caste. When he had to bring my ailing mother to Surat by road, he spent Rs 300 for porters, torches and transportation.

There is much else to write about, but time does not permit it. In thirty-seven years, he earned Rs 25,000 through sheer hard work. He paid off Rs 2,000, which was his one-third share of his father's debt. He single-handedly bore the cost of all the rituals on the occasions of the birth of his first child, my own birth, my two weddings, the birth of my firstborn, my mother's death and the death of my wife. When he died, he left behind for me by way of inheritance a promissory note for Rs 5,000, bearing an interest of 4 per cent, ornaments worth Rs 1,000, a two-room house which was worth Rs 2,000 (building cost Rs 1,200, cost of repairs Rs 600 and Rs 200 being the cost of land) and other miscellaneous articles worth Rs 500.

My mother, Navdurga, was called Nani by most, although her in-laws addressed her as Rukmani Vahu. She was born in the month of Aso of Samvat 1875 and died at the age of thirty-three on Kartik Vad 4, Samvat 1907. She was industrious, tidy, contented, thrifty and a skilled homemaker. She knew how to read and write. She was also accomplished at needlework and singing. She had a gentle and affable disposition, but ruled over me with an iron fist as a child. She had compassion for her poorer relatives and would often help them by giving them things such as clothes etc. When she felt lonely, she would sometimes weep at the memory of her departed loved ones. She was devout and observed her rituals faithfully. She never turned away anyone seeking alms. Once, however, a fake sadhu came to our home when my father was at work and requested some snuff. My father gave it to him. The sadhu then began to blow bubbles from his mouth (people said it was his entrails) and apparently squeezed out water from some grains of rice. My father was impressed and came in to ask for clothes—a dhoti and an *angarkha*—to give to the sadhu. My mother, unfazed, emerged from the kitchen and drove away the sadhu. Till date, I do not know what came over my father that day—he wasn't a gullible man. I remember how, during my mother's final illness, she would call me and ask me to lay my head on her aching stomach. I would do so, slightly abashed at performing this childlike gesture as an adult. I cannot forget the image of her gently shedding tears of love (alas, those were her final days!).

These, then, are some facts about my parents. No words can do justice to their nobility, and such words would be considered exaggeration by the world. My heartfelt desire is that just as I have been happy with my parents, so may other young children be happy with theirs.

Viram 3

1833–45

1. My birth was a painful one for my mother (Navdurga, called Nani by most and Rukmani Vahu by her in-laws). At the time of birth, my head was rather long and my appearance rather strange (of course, now my head has acquired its normal roundish shape). In six months, I had learnt to crawl on my knees.

2. About ten months or so after my birth, my mother and I, accompanied by my mother's uncle Dullabhram, went to Bombay, where my father was stationed. I learnt to speak at the age of two. Until then, I could eat no solids and survived on milk and mashed food.

3. When the Great Fire occurred in Samvat 1893, I was in Bombay. I remember rather distinctly that I was playing in the drawing room of our home in Bhagwan

Kala building when one of our neighbours, a Vaniya named Dayaram Bhukhan, came rushing in at about noon. He seemed greatly agitated. 'All of Surat has burnt down,' he exclaimed. Hearing him, the women tenants in the building who came from Surat (the men, naturally, were at work) were stunned into silence. Those words, 'All of Surat has burnt down', still ring in my ears.

4. The task of reconstruction of the burnt houses that were destroyed in the Vaishakh of Samvat 1893 was finally completed in Samvat 1895. During that period, my mother and I spent some time in Surat. I remember an incident that occurred during this time. While playing with my cousin on the ground opposite our house, I chucked a stone at my cousin and he was hurt. My aunt complained, and my mother, in a fit of anger, thrashed me, tied me to the handle of a large wooden chest and locked me up in the staircase room. I kept screaming and shouting. Hearing my shouts, our help Govan Gajjar took pity on me and let me out. I still remember this incident.

On another occasion, in Bombay, I had broken a pot of oil, and at that time too, my mother had given me a thrashing. My father, on returning from work that evening, tried to make peace between us. I argued back, and he too slapped me. These were the only occasions when I was beaten up.

5. When I turned five, my father enrolled me in Nana Mehta's school near Bhuleshwar. At that time, other students were invited to our home and given jaggery and parched grain to celebrate the event. I have memories of us students saying 'Sarasti, Sarasti (Goddess Sarasvati), you are my mother' and 'Jee, Mehtaji, salamat'. I also remember how, at night, some of us would get together and memorize tables by reciting them aloud at the top of our voices. While in Surat, I used to attend Ichchha Mehta and Fakir Mehta's school.

6. By and large, I kept in good health in my childhood save when I was about seven. I had a tapeworm infection and was laid up for about six months.

7. At the age of eight, in the Vaishakh of Samvat 1897, I had my sacred thread ceremony. After this, I began learning the *sandhya*, *rudri* and Vedas on the one hand and, on the other, I began attending the government Gujarati school. I learnt the Vedas from Balaji, a

Marathi friend of my father's. I learnt two sections from him and then the rest from another Maharashtrian till I completed one cluster of eight. That is the limit of my formal learning of the Vedas. I remember, once, there was a sacred ritual celebration at my kaka's home. The Brahmins were reciting mantras for a particular ritual. I was asked to join in, and so I did. My recitation was praised later. This was when I was about ten years old.

I was initially enrolled in Balgovind Mehtaji's school in Pydhonie in Bombay. Shortly after, I came to Surat and was enrolled in Durgaram Mehta's school located in Navalsha's *kotha* in Nanavat, Surat. I can still visualize the grandeur of that school. And if the place itself inspired awe, naturally, Mehtaji inspired even more awe—nay, fear itself. I could pronounce my consonants well, but every time Mehtaji tested me, in fear, I would make a mistake in enunciating the letter 'anga' and would fail the examination. I spent almost a month in the section where we were to learn consonants. One day, Dolatram Vakil, who was related to us on my mother's side, learnt of this and was quite upset. He felt that my pronunciations were perfect and that Mehtaji was unnecessarily holding me back. He decided to accompany me and confront Mehtaji. Mehtaji made me go through the enunciation of 'anga', and I could do so perfectly. Mehtaji declared me passed and I moved on. Ah, how rigorous was the method of teaching in those days, unlike the casual and shallow methods adopted today!

8. On the Vaishakh Sud 12 of Samvat 1900, 29 April 1844, I married the daughter of Surajram, a law officer of the Sudder Court in Surat.

9. The credit for my education in Gujarati goes to Balgovind Mehtaji. It was after learning from him that I went on to appear for my examination in Gujarati before John Harkness, principal of Elphinstone School. I was enrolled in the English school on 6 January 1845. I also remember an incident from my Surat days. I had heard that an award had been declared for a competition. I admitted myself to Pranshankar Mehta's school and won the award—the book *Balmitra*.

10. I studied for about 3.5 years in the government school, but my attendance was irregular since I would spend some time in Bombay and some in Surat. In Bombay, too, I had won some books as awards in various

competitions. In Balgovind's school, I secured the first or second rank in my class.

11. During that period, the books that I read were as follows: *Balmitra*, Nityanand-Parmanand's *Geography–Astronomy*, Aesop's *Fables*, *The Story of Daadasli*, *Panchopaakhyaan*, *Bodhvachan*, *Lipidhaara*, Gangadhar Shastri's book on grammar and the first part of *Ganit Shikshamala*.

When I read *Balmitra* and Nityanand-Parmanand, a sense of wondrous pleasure would envelop my mind. Nityanand-Parmanand's chapters on astronomy were particularly fascinating. From *Balmitra*, I remember clearly being moved by the chapter on the monsoon, the tree of thorns, the nobility of the old mother in the story of the little girl who picked grains, the story of little Jagu and the character of the king in the story of Antik.

12. During those three and a half years, despite my shuttling between Bombay and Surat, my interest in learning at school never flagged. In addition, I also read the Vedas and other books at home. As soon as I woke up, I would go through one page of *Balmitra*

in detail, analysing and understanding the grammatical rules involved, and only then would I clean my teeth. In Bombay, I would play with the neighbours' children only for a short time in the evening.

13. Among my friends was a neighbour and fellow member of my caste, Parbhuram. Later in life, he acquired a very good command over Gujarati and taught Gujarati to many Englishmen. He was my closest friend, and we would spend time together, studying together and going to school together. Once we did some mischief at home, and Parbhuram's father informed Balgovind of this. Mehtaji made us hold each other's ears and do squats as punishment. I remember that incident clearly.

14. When I was in the first grade of Balgovind's school, I followed a silly and superstitious ritual—I would unlock the door to the school, stand before the map of the world, shut my eyes and try to place my finger on the Sandwich and Society Islands in the Pacific Ocean. I would then open my eyes to see if I had done that correctly. I believed that if I placed my finger on the correct location, I would stand first in the class—and that was mostly the case.

15. As a child, I was not rambunctious but rather serious by temperament. Yet, if I didn't get my own way, I would sulk in a corner and quietly shed tears—not flail and wail. I was timid and would seek to hide in a corner or behind my mother in the presence of strangers. The relatives on my mother's side called me *shankariyo*.

16. I remember that when my mother and I were in Surat (my father was, at the time, in Bombay), we used to sleep on a large chest. One night of Aso Sud 1, I woke up at midnight screaming in terror. My mother immediately got up and clasped me to her chest. My uncle Ichchhashankar, who was with us, smeared some holy ash on me and recited a chapter of the *Chandipaath*. From that day, I was gripped by such fear that I would refuse to sleep at home. My mother took me at nights to various relatives' homes to sleep, but the same thing would happen there. One night, I was sleeping in the front room at the home of my mother's aunt. I woke up at midnight to drink water. When I sat up on the bed, I felt that someone was trying to open the door. I turned on my face and tried to sleep but woke up screaming in fear once again. My aunt's landlord, Lalbhai, who was said to be

able to exorcise spirits, did something. All I remember is seeing a walking stick near the lamp that night. Although I remember the incident, I do not quite know how old I was at the time. Later, when I met my mother's aunt, she asked me if I still remembered the incident, and I said I did. On inquiring, she told me that I was five or six years old at the time.

17. I used to suffer from nightmares—only over the last eight years or so have they stopped occurring frequently. I tried to maintain a written record of those dreams whenever I remembered them; I did so in order to understand why they occurred. But I wasn't able to maintain this record for long. 'An enemy king's army has entered the city with flaring torches and blaring bugles—the roads are lit up with lamps—there is commotion in the town—people are locking themselves up in their homes—the invaders are wreaking destruction everywhere—shouts, screams all around—people are frozen into inaction out of fear—don't kill the children, the parents plead—they hide their ornaments. I cover my eyes with my hands and take refuge in my mother's side' etc.

'On the way to Bombay from Surat, there is a wide creek—ghosts arrive and swirl around—the waters of the creek rise—I drown' etc.

'An elephant is chasing me and I desperately try to run, but I can't—I imagine I am leaping on to his back—but now the elephant is really close—I shut my eyes in fear and fall down to the ground' and so on. In the *Pingal*, I have written a line, 'Efforts will drive away even the most evil thoughts.' This was inspired by this dream in which I made desperate efforts to escape from the elephant.

'I have gone to bathe in the Tapi late on a moonlit night—I see a fair, innocent-looking child—filled with pity, I go near—it grows larger and larger—suddenly it turns towards me and I now see it is a demon glaring at me with its fearsome eyes—in fright, I collapse to the ground—it bursts into flames and disappears!'

I had heard many tales of appeasing various spirits, Kali and Bhairav, and these also shaped my nightmares. Just last year, when I was grieving the loss of a loved one, I came across the Richardson selection. I read the last section of *Othello* and that night I dreamt thus: 'I was being crushed by a demon—I had heard of boas crushing the bones of buffaloes. I said to the demon,

"Go ahead, demon, kill me if you think it's a great feat of valour.'"

For some reason, the thought occurred to me that the day of death was predestined and nothing could change that.* My eyes flew open. My body was curled into a foetal position, and I couldn't speak for a while. These are examples of the kind of nightmares that I suffered from. I still dream, but now my dreams are not frightening ones. They are about my doing great deeds. I wrote the poem 'Niti Tumbi Bhavsindhu Ne Taraave' (Ethics and Intentions Are the Raft That Navigate the Ocean of Life) inspired by a dream of a sinking ship.

---

* I was a very timid child, but once, at age eighteen, I came to the realization that my death would occur on its predestined date and in the predestined manner. From that moment, I lost my fear of ghosts and other unpleasant things. But before then, it was another matter. In Bombay, we had to descend two levels of staircases and go to a dark, unlit area to answer calls of nature. I used to fear that a ghost would attack me there. In Surat, the wife of one of our tenants was said to suffer possession by spirits, and I refused to go to the third floor, where she lived. I would take care not to relieve myself below a banyan or peepal tree. Today (1866), of course, I don't believe in ghosts and spirits.

18. My mother and I often travelled between Surat and Bombay by road. Whether it was summer, winter or monsoon, we took the road that went through the forests and along the coast. Travel by boat did not suit us, and we preferred travelling on foot or by carriage. Those days of travel as a child have left a strong imprint on my memory. Once my mother and I were travelling from Valsad to Dungri during the high monsoon season, and we fell off the bullock into the mud. We had to spend the night at a fisherman's hut in Dungri. Often, the other men travelling in our group would prefer to walk, plucking drumstick flowers, khaakhra leaves, mangoes and tamarind pods from trees along the way. At the dharamshalas, we would eat different types of khichdi with ghee. While food was being cooked at the dharamshala, I would loiter around the area swinging a stick in my hand, or sit by the well. The image of the evening light filtering through the canopy of trees and the village well, its parapet grooved by ropes, is fresh in my mind's eye even today. I also remember the heat and humidity of the forests that we walked through. Once, we almost drowned in the Mahim creek. I remember the feelings that arose in me at the sight of the sea while travelling on a sailboat. When

travelling by a steamer from Surat to Bombay, the sight of the cape in Bombay would suddenly energize me. The sight of the large buildings in Fort on the way home from the port would fill me with wonder. I still remember how, when on a steamer from Bombay to Surat, the very air seemed to change at Valsad. These memories became sharper and even more gloriously vivid when I started writing my poetry. Alas, I can no longer replicate the sense of wonder at the novelty of things that I saw during my travels in childhood. I can only understand it intellectually.

19. As a child, I did not play much with others of my age. In Surat, I would venture out with other children but rarely participated in their play, preferring to stand alone and observe. I never had much interest in games. Even today (1866), I can only play all versions of *sokta* (Indian version of ludo) really well and chess only moderately so.

Viram 4

1845–51

1. I was admitted to an English school at the age of eleven years and four months on 6 January 1845. My first teacher was Master Shaikhmohammed. He wasn't a learned man but was humble and a sincere teacher. He taught me McClerk's *First Reading* and *Second Reading* for almost a year. After this, Master Bomanji Pestonjee, who is now in England in the commerce department, taught me *Third Reading*, The Moral Classbook, *A Series of Lessons* and *A Course of Reading* and *Geography*. He was a gregarious man and an effective teacher. After this, for the scholarship candidates' class, I had as my teachers Mr Graham and Mr Reid. Mr Graham taught algebra and geometry, and Mr Reid taught Taylor's *Ancient and Modern History*, Marshman's *India*, poetry and composition.

52

Thanks to his entertaining and light-hearted manner of teaching, we felt no burden in attending his classes. Mr Graham, on the other hand, was considered tough by the students. He would sometimes mock them, but I do not remember being reprimanded by him. I always stood first in his class.

For an intervening period, we had one Blackwell, a bit of a blockhead, who taught us mathematics. I never got along with him. Once, I had solved an equation in a simpler manner but not as per the method shown in the textbook. Not only did he mark it incorrect, but asked me to stand outside the classroom. Just then, Mr McDougal, a professor of mathematics, arrived. I complained to him. He had a look at my slate and told Blackwell that my solution was absolutely correct and that I had actually demonstrated my intelligence. Blackwell's fallen face was worth looking at.

I had always learnt my arithmetic by reading aloud as well as writing in English. I had managed to reach up to the stage of fractions. Suddenly, McDougal decided to teach algebra to a small group of students. To that end, he conducted an examination and those who did not perform well had to learn only arithmetic and that too, in Gujarati. I had made a mistake in my sum, and so I too was consigned to the arithmetic lot. McDougal was quite a sight—a squat figure, small, bespectacled eyes, swaying like an elephant as he walked. He was rather fond of snuff and was a kind and simple man.

Having learnt the abovementioned subjects from the abovementioned teachers for five years and two months, I appeared for the Clare Scholarship examination in April 1850.

2. During this period of my education, I used to derive a strange sense of joy when I read descriptions of nations, natural phenomena and poetry. What must those nations be like! How different must be the ways of those people! Reading poetry fired my imagination and perhaps was responsible for the first flowering of my creative ability. Of course, this was fleeting since I was young and inexperienced. Ah, the sense of wonder that filled me when I read Taylor's *Ancient History*! Reading about the Egyptians, the descriptions of their lives, the pyramids and the Nile—such marvels! That sense of wonder experienced in childhood and that joy are incomparable. I do feel joy even today when I read those same descriptions or even poetry, but it is not the same.

3. I remember an incident that occurred during the scholarship exam. The examiner, Patton, had shortlisted some problems (without their solutions). A Parsi, Mancherjee (who is today a teacher in Jamshedji's school), picked them up from his table and gave them to his friend Mayaram Shambhunath a day before the examination in the hope that Mayaram could provide the answers. Mayaram had been a close friend of mine since the days when we were learning *Second Reading* and is my friend even today. He is today a deputy inspector. Mayaram brought them over to my place, and we worked till late in the night, solving most of the problems. The next day, in the exam, of all the students, Mayaram and I had managed to solve the highest number of problems.

4. I derived the same pleasure from solving algebraic equations and problems in geometry as I did from reading English books, perhaps more. I would try to find new methods to solve these problems. Unlike many who hate mathematics because they find it difficult, I enjoyed coming up with new solutions to mathematical problems. This aptitude increased with practice. What logical ability I have today I attribute

largely to my early love for algebra and geometry. It would give me great joy when I managed to find a new method or new proof to an algebraic equation or geometric principle. I wasn't interested in improving my handwriting or memorizing facts in history and geography, but was more focused on spelling, grammar and parsing sentences.

5. I have never been reprimanded for missing my lessons. I always maintained a rank between one and five in my class. In December 1849, for my performance in a competitive examination, I was awarded a prize of books worth Rs 16: Taylor's *Ancient History*, Herschel's *Astronomy* and Chamber's *Geometry and Trigonometry*. I do not recollect ever being punished or beaten for misbehaving in class except once, when for some reason that I do not remember, I received two strokes of the cane from Dr Bhau in a writing class. Mr Navrojee Fardunjee, Dr Bhau Daji and Mr Bhogilal Pranvallabhdas were awe-inspiring figures in those days. Such was the grandeur of my school!

6. When I was learning *A Series of Lessons*, the governor visited our school. I read aloud in his presence the piece

on the Fiery Courser from poems of natural history. The governor was pleased and declared, 'The boy exhibits his comprehension in the way he reads.' But I did not quite understand the meaning of the piece then. This just goes to show how, merely through assiduous practice, one can read as if one has understood the meaning of what is being read.

7. My father had not hired a private tutor to teach me English lessons; I learnt them on my own. Our teacher Bamanji would not provide translations in advance. I would sit at home with a dictionary and manage a half-baked translation. In school the next day, some of us would work together and prepare a more polished version. In class, as the lesson progressed, matters would become clearer still. We would work at our lessons even during the half-hour break that we got.

8. In addition to this English education, I used to learn the *Saraswat* daily for two hours in the morning from an Audichya shastri named Ambashankar. I do not quite recollect the exact period for which I did this, but I do know that I learnt one and a half sections from the Saraswat. Ambashankar was a dignified and humble man.

9. I would wake up with my father at 4 a.m. every day. I would go over the lesson that I had finished the previous night; I wouldn't do any new work. Then I would practice my Sanskrit. I would then go to Ambashankar. I would return at eight, bathe and perform the Sandhya Puja. For some time, I used to perform Shiva Puja also. My father and I would eat at nine thirty. We would sit for a while. I would then have paan, dress and leave for school at ten thirty. On returning at five thirty, I would go to the terrace to enjoy some fresh air and finally, when the lamps were lit, I would sit to work at my lessons. I would have my supper at eight thirty and once again sit to study from nine to ten thirty. In the month of Shravan, I would go to the Mahadev temple for puja. I also followed the dietary restrictions as prescribed on days such as Janmashtami, Shivaratri and other auspicious days.

10. I was so superstitious that if I so much as suspected that a drop of someone's spittle had touched my face, I would rub at it with my angarkha till I almost bled. On the way to school, I would stop at Kalkadevi's temple for *darshan*. I would beseech her 'O mother, I am a sinner, forgive me and bless me'. I would then slap myself. This

was not so that I would get a high rank in my class, but it had become a habit born of my devotion. One day, I was slapping myself when a carpenter saw me and said, 'Hit harder!' From that day, I was embarrassed to slap myself openly. After paying my respects to the goddess, I would furtively glance about to make sure no one was looking. I would then gently tap myself with my right hand while covering it with my left. There is a Shiva temple named Narmadeshwar in Bombay, which is not very popular among devotees. I would offer oblations in the dark and would prostrate myself saying, 'I am a sinner.' If I went to the Ramji temple, I would perform several circumambulations. This overt devotion and later my melancholia in adult life were perhaps inherited from my mother. She never explicitly asked me to express my devotion in this manner, but I could see that it pleased her.

11. In our days, there were four levels of scholarships for college education—the Clare, worth ten rupees, the Uwest, worth fifteen, Second Normal, worth twenty and First Normal, worth thirty rupees. There were several candidates for the Clare, among which eleven passed. I ranked third among them. The examiners

were Principal Henry Green, Professor Patton, Thomas Reid and two other Englishmen. The exam was held in April 1850, but due to the vacation in May, I joined college in June. I had managed to attempt many of the questions in almost all the subjects, but there was one essay in English where I drew a blank. I wrote one paragraph and managed to get seven marks. In the history composition class, I had written many long essays reasonably well, but the topic of that essay was whether or not education for women is beneficial. My lack of worldliness, largely due to my complete focus on book learning, was the reason I couldn't write that essay.

12. I do not clearly remember my textbooks in college, but I do remember that Patton taught us mathematics— harmonics, polar algebra and trigonometry. Dr Gyro taught us chemistry, lectures as well as laboratory, and Green taught us political economy and logic.

13. I, along with some fellow students from my college and a couple of other friends, used to perform chemistry experiments at home. We decided to pool our books and establish a small library in my house. We then decided

to meet four times in a month. For two of those days, we would read out to the others essays that we had written in advance and discuss the ideas presented in them. It would sharpen our oral communication and debating skills. For the other two days, we decided to hold public meetings and spread ideas of social reform among the public at large. We decide to call our meetings 'Juvaan Purushoni Anyoanya Buddhivardhak Sabha' (Young Men's Society for Mutual Intellectual Advancement). I was the president, Mayaram Shambhunath the secretary, Kalyanji Shivlal the treasurer and Narandas Kalyandas and two others were office-bearers. The public lectures were held before an audience of 100 persons in an empty building in Bhuleshwar Chakla that belonged to an acquaintance of our friends Meghji and Bhavani Laxman. I delivered my speech on the benefits of forming associations, and Bhai Narandas presented a lecture on magic. Later, we changed the location to the Panjrapole building, thanks to our friend Bhai Harilal, whose father Mohanlal was an administrative clerk of the Panjrapole. Bhai Maneklal Gopaldas had written an essay to promote education for women and had submitted it to the office-bearers for scrutiny, but before we could decide on a date for presenting it to the public, I had to leave for Surat.*

14. In July–August 1850, a friend of mine wrote a letter to me from Surat. Some of the contents were of a confidential nature regarding my relations with women. Although it had my name as recipient, the postal address was that of my father-in-law, Surajram, shastri of Sudder Court. My father-in-law, assuming it was meant for him, opened it and read it. Realizing it was meant for me, he instructed someone to 'deliver it to Narmadashankar'. Meanwhile, another letter arrived, similarly addressed. This too was read by my father-in-law. I had already written to my friend asking him not to send letters in this manner. This friend of mine also happened to be my father-in-law's nephew (his sister's son). My father-in-law was furious after reading the first letter and informed the young man's family in Surat. As a result, my friend was thrashed by

---

* Ten–fifteen days after my departure for Surat, Bhai Pranlal, Bhai Mohanlal and others came to the Panjrapole hoping to be amused at the antics of youth. But the members of the sabha requested them to join the sabha. They assented and the name of the group was changed to Buddhivardhak Hindu Sabha.—31 March 1851.

his father. Unable to bear this humiliation, my friend, who was employed as a teacher, quit his job saying he had better prospects elsewhere and left Surat. When he returned to Surat two years later, I embraced him at the Havadiya Chakla in the presence of others. I was disgusted at my father-in-law's behaviour. Being a well-ranked officer, could he not have read the address before opening the letters meant for me? I drafted a stiff letter reprimanding him, but my father advised me against sending it, and I tore it up.

15. Once I joined college, there were no lessons to be prepared at home (no homework is assigned in college; one simply has to attend the lectures delivered by professors). I therefore spent my time reading various books in English. However, I kept away from novels and tales.

16. In September 1850, my youth began to assert itself. Although I had stayed away from bad company, and despite the fact that I had never read any books about sexual relations, a new set of emotions surged through my mind—I could sense the scent of women. There were several other tenants in the complex that we lived in. I began to eavesdrop on the conversations of the

tenants' wives. I was curious to know what the women did in their own time. I began to read the stories of Shamalbhatt. All this should have aroused sexual desire in me, but it did not. What it did arouse was the desire to have a romantic relationship with a woman. I was always shy, and besides, I had no friends who were experienced in matters of romance. So I could not act upon my desire. I kept hoping that some woman would take the first step. These desires would usually bubble forth during the holidays, when I was alone at home—and that too during the day, never at night. These feelings persisted for a few months, but I was not weighed down by them.

17. On 23 November 1850, my mother died in Surat. My father was with her at the time, and I was alone in Bombay. When the news of her death reached Gokulnath, my father's friend, I was teaching a Parsi in the Fort area. When I returned at 11 a.m., I saw Gokulnath sitting on the veranda of my home. He stopped me from climbing the stairs to my room—I immediately understood. I cast aside my turban and, in shocked silence, sat down beside him on the veranda.

18. In my life so far, this was the first tragic death among
    my kin or my family that I was experiencing—my
    own mother's death. That my father was not around
    to console me made my grief even more unbearable.
    During the period of mourning, I did not attend
    college. All I did for those ten days was to sit at the
    window of my third-floor room all day and stare out—
    even the sun seemed to weep, and its light seemed pale.
    The nights were as bad. The sadness that enveloped
    me was a sadness of renunciation, not death. My
    thoughts dwelt on bodily disease, the fear of death
    and God. Every now and then, I mumbled to myself,
    'Let Krishna do what he wants. Why, O mind, do
    you live in worry?'* After the thirteenth-day rites,
    I resumed college, but found that I could not
    concentrate. This state of mind persisted for more
    than a month.

19. After a fortnight, I received a letter from Surat. It
    was to the effect that since his wife was now of age,
    Narmadashankar should come soon. My father-in-

---

* I did not know then that this was written by Dayaram. At the time,
they were only stray words of a *bhajan* that my mother used to sing.

law desired that I should set up home in Surat. My father was of two minds. Surat would be convenient, but Bombay was a better choice in terms of educational opportunities. It would also mean that father and son could stay together. At the time, I was keen on meeting my wife. Suddenly, I had an attack of cholera, and so my father decided to send me to Surat. My father-in-law was making efforts through his friend Vinayakrao, the son of Jagannath Sankarsett, to get a recommendation sent to Mr Graham, who was in charge of the school in Surat, to secure a position for me there. By now, I really did want to be in Surat. I was sure that due to my poor attendance, I would not pass the college examination, and a job in Surat would be ideal.

20. Although I had almost recovered from my illness, I used it as an excuse, and having secured certificates from my professors, I quit college and came to Surat. The certificates that I received are as under:

1

Elphinstone Institution
Feb 8th 1851

I have known Narmadashankar for the last eighteen months; but principally, since June 1850, at which period he commenced his studies in the College Department of the Elphinstone Institution. Out of a large list of candidates for Clare Scholarships, of whom eleven succeeded, Narmadashankar obtained the third place. He distinguished throughout the term as a student but has lately been attacked by cholera, which has left him so weak and ill that his doctor insists upon his removal from Bombay to his native town, Surat.

We all part with him with great regret.

(Signed) H. GREEN
Acting Principal

2

Narmadashankar Lalshankar, a student in the College Department of the Elphinstone Institution, has been under my tuition in English literature and history for the last year and a half. It would be impossible to speak too highly of his acquirements, or of his industry. His knowledge of the English language is remarkably good for his standing, and he has made considerable progress in the study of history, ancient and modern, but more particularly in the history of India. At the examinations of June 1849 [1850] he came out 3rd in his class and was appointed a Clare or 1st year's scholar, in which capacity he has given great satisfaction and I regret to say that he is now obliged to leave (I hope only for the present) Bombay.

He is decidedly a boy of great talents and his conduct as far as I know of has been always most unexceptionable.

Elphinstone Institution   (Signed) R.T. REID A.B
February 14th 1851   Acting Professor of History
                                 and General Literature

3*

I have great pleasure in bearing testimony to the good conduct and industry of Narmadashankar Lalshankar since I became acquainted with him. At the scholarship

---

* Patton was too busy at the time to write this certificate, and I left for Surat without it. It was subsequently sent to me by my father.

examination in April 1850 his answering was extremely good and his progress since has been very fair notwithstanding his ill health, which I regret has at last compelled him to leave the Institution.

Elphinstone Institution   JOSEPH PATTON
25th Feby 1851   *Profr Math and Physics*

Viram 5

1851–54

1. I arrived in Surat on 19 February 1851. After a few days, I visited the head of the Surat school, Mr Graham. I inquired of him whether he had received any communication concerning me from Vinayakrao Jagannath. He acknowledged that he had, but there was a board resolution to the effect that a salary raise was to be given to the teachers who were at the Surat school. It had been decided by the board that those monitors employed at a salary of three or four rupees would be laid off, and only six monitors would be retained at a higher salary. I was disappointed. I put my case to Graham, that I had been a student of his at the school and so my case deserved some consideration. He told me to keep following up. I enrolled myself in the first class at the school in the hope of securing a job,

but my attendance was irregular, and finally I gave up attending altogether.

2. With my father in Bombay, I found myself unemployed and alone. I sank into a state of self-pity, and I found my thoughts dwelling on my mother and her absence. At this time, I formed a relationship with a wise and noble woman, and that offered me solace.

3. To make constructive use of my time, I thought of establishing a society and put forth my proposal to my friend Dolatram. He suggested that in addition to the society, we should also start some publishing activities. In partnership with him, I established a society, Swadesh Hitechchhu (Well-Wishers of the Nation). From a printing press nearby, we began to bring out a weekly newspaper, *Gyansagar* (Ocean of Knowledge). We also began to organize lectures. Dolatram's motive behind starting *Gyansagar* was to expose certain actions of Durgaram Mehtaji, but I came to know of this only much later. I wrote out my first lecture on 'The Benefits of Forming Associations' and delivered it on 4 July. *Gyansagar* lasted for about one year. Then the society disintegrated.

4. In that year, my wife had a miscarriage in her third month.

5. The teacher at Rander's government Gujarati school was not performing well. So Mr Graham dismissed him and appointed me in his place from 1 May 1852 onwards at a salary of Rs 15. I accepted the offer, since it was better than doing nothing.

6. I would wake up at 4 in the morning and take the boat to cross the river.* If I had made arrangements the previous day, a horse would be waiting and I would ride to the school. If not, I would try to arrange for a horse, and if those efforts proved fruitless, I would walk to the school, a good two hours' journey. I would reach Rander at 7.30–8. I would eat something and, being exhausted, take a nap. There were a couple of older boys from rich families who were my students of First Class (Senior Division) and who had great affection for me. They helped me in running the school. They had appointed one student from each *mohalla* whose responsibility it was to make sure that

---

* I would handle the rudder while the boatman handled the sail. Ah, what joy it was to sail in the rain during the monsoon!

students from that *mohalla* attended school. Due to this, all the students would arrive at the school by 6 in the morning. The Senior Division students would be monitors for the other classes and would teach there. I would finish my nap by 9 a.m. and would attend each class for 5–10–15 minutes. At 10 a.m., I would dismiss the junior students and would teach the senior students of the First Class till 11.30. I would then go to bathe in the Tapi, where I would enjoy myself till about two. I would head back and have lunch at three. The school would have resumed classes 2 p.m. onwards, and the monitors would be conducting classes. After lunch, I would attend each class for a short time and dismiss the junior classes at 4.30. I would once again teach the students of First Class for an hour. I would take a boat back if it was available. Otherwise, I would walk along the riverbank, enjoying the beauty of nature, and arrive home at about 7. I would have my supper and go to sleep. In this manner, I single-handedly managed to teach eighty students. There was a Jain boy, Bhaichand, who, under my tutelage, had become quite an expert in geometry. Kalyandas's and Vajubhai Parekh's children had also become quite proficient in reading and writing. Occasionally, I would travel to the villages surrounding Rander. Before examinations, I would stay in Rander and take extra lessons for the children. It so happened that once, Mr Graham landed up in Rander without prior intimation. The children had just spread their mats and were getting set for class when he arrived and sat on the chair. I used to stay in a room adjoining the classrooms. As I emerged from the room, Graham chided me for being lazy. I simply replied that I worked till late in the night, and anyway, he had failed to inform us of his arrival in advance. How could I be expected to make any preparations? He conducted a spot examination by asking students questions. He was impressed by their replies and informed the few people who had by now gathered that they had a good teacher. They should make use of this opportunity while it was available and send their children to study.

7. The commute to Rander was getting too much for me, and I began searching for a job in Surat. It so happened that Durgaram Mehta and Mr Graham had some differences, and Durgaram Mehta was transferred to Rajkot. Tripurashankar, who ran the Nanpara school, was appointed in his place, and I was given charge of the

Nanpara school in March 1853. The children from this school shifted to the new school with Tripurashankar. So it fell to my lot to start from scratch. But thanks to my reputation, children from Katargam and even from Rander (those who were fond of me) came all the way to Nanpara to learn. Eventually, I became disenchanted with this job. Not many were keen to learn, there was not much to teach, and to top it all, a teacher's position had little prestige in society. I applied to the resident of Baroda, Mr Fulljames, for a job, but did not get any response.

8. In Samvat 1908, my wife had her first successful pregnancy, and a girl was born to us in July or August 1852, but died within fifteen days of her birth. My wife conceived again in Samvat 1909 but had a stillborn child at eight months. Due to complications from this delivery, she too died at the age of sixteen or seventeen, on 4 October 1853.[*]

---

[*] Once, during her pregnancy, she was going to her maternal home and saw a black snake along the way. This filled her with terror. I am sure that she caught a fever that day and that finally led to her death. I had myself gone to bury our baby in the morning. I cannot forget the

sight of that tender fair creature while I placed it in the grave. I could not bear to pour earth into the grave. I returned from burying my child, only to make preparations for cremating my wife! At 3 that afternoon, I went back 3 miles to cremate her. There are many rituals that have to be performed before cremating a woman who has just delivered a child. She is laid out in a shallow pit, water is sprinkled and mantras chanted etc. The sight of my wife at that time—her unbraided tresses, her vermillion-smeared forehead, her fair complexion with her eyes shut—I cannot forget that ever! How many creatures inhabiting the sands of the river must have died that evening in the pyre! She was called Nanigauri in her maternal home and Gulabvahu in my home. She was short and very fair. There were faint pockmarks on her face from a childhood attack of smallpox. But her fair face shone from a distance. She hadn't studied much, nor was she particularly skilled at housework, but she was innocent, obedient and loved me greatly. It was said in my community that I gave her a difficult time, but the reality was this: I would return home only at 9–10 p.m., and she would have spent all that time alone in the house. The women of her maternal home would poison her ears with rumours about me, and perhaps she suffered from bouts of jealousy and suspicion on that account. But she never expressed those feelings in front of me. Similarly, coming from a rich home and being clumsy, she caused much damage by dropping and breaking things at home. But I never complained nor scolded her on that account. It is true that her extreme innocence and the fact that she wasn't educated dimmed my love for her. I did not get along well with my father-in-law. He did not like my active role in the reform movement. In my lecture on the benefits of forming associations, I had come down rather heavily on shastris, and that had upset him greatly.

9. After the death of my wife, I was all alone in my house. There was constant pressure to keep enrolment high in the school. I tried for better, more reputable jobs, but was unsuccessful. This depressed me even further. I had had my fill of worldly affairs and obligations. Once again, the desire to achieve great intellectual heights stirred in me—much like when I was learning English. This gave further impetus to the idea of moving to Bombay. Surat was now unbearable. I wrote a letter in English to Principal Harkness, to the effect that I had tasted the fruit of learning and the taste had forever stayed with me. I requested him to give me a part-time job as a teacher of Gujarati so that I could spend the remaining time pursuing my study

---

Once, when the subject of social reform came up in the presence of others, he had said, 'Nothing will ever remove this blot.' I had said to him, 'If you do not have the capability to find faults in our arguments, it is not our problem. To not engage with us and then to grumble behind our back is not right.' I may not have got along with my father-in-law, but he was an icon of respectability among the Nagars of Surat. His reputation was much enhanced by his position as a shastri in the Sudder Court at a salary of Rs 300. My mother-in-law had a lot of affection for me, but the house was ruled by the other women, especially my sisters-in-law, who constantly poisoned my wife's ears. I, too, had a very low opinion of them. My mother developed a dislike for them on the day of my engagement itself.

of English. I received no response, and my frustration grew. Finally, the urge to go to Bombay grew so strong that on 29 October 1853, I wrote a letter of resignation to Graham saying, 'Certain extenuating circumstances at home compel me to resign with immediate effect from my position as a teacher and move to Bombay. I am hopeful that you may treat this as my notice and relieve me as soon as the statutory notice period is over.' I received the reply, 'Apply again with a three-month notice period.' I wrote that it was impossible for me to stay for such a long period and requested that I may be relieved. I finally received an order from Kheda on 27 December: 'In view of your representation, your resignation has been accepted and you may hand over charge to the teacher at Rander.' On 2 January 1854, I handed over charge to the teacher at Rander—my brother-in-law Keshavram—and on the very next day, boarded a steamer for Bombay.

10. From 19 February 1851 to 2 January 1854, I hadn't read a single book—neither in Gujarati nor in English; and save for one letter to Harkness, I hadn't written a word in English. Except for about three speeches in Gujarati, I hadn't written anything else. I made no contributions to *Gyansagar*; it was all Dolatram's writing. I drank

bhang, consumed opium and enjoyed the company of women. In my solitary moments, I would dream of earning fame (never money) and of being in a romantic relationship. I never articulated any ideas of reform, whether in private or public. In fact, I never even dreamt of reforms regarding caste discrimination, remarriage, idol worship and food restrictions. My idea of reforms was restricted to working diligently, maintaining social harmony, delivering speeches, reading essays, writing books and striving for the betterment of the nation.

I had befriended Jaduram, the publisher of *Gyansagar*. He would sometimes talk of the number of syllables in *dohra* or *chopai*, which I would listen to only perfunctorily. During the month of Bhadarva, I would go to see the celebrations and would hear verses being recited, but they never drew my attention. My primary purpose was to enjoy the company of friends.

In those days, Dalpatram Kavi* was in Surat, and I knew him from afar, as in, this is Dalpatram

---

* Two incidents that occurred during that period were narrated to me later by my friends. Durgaram Mehtaji had praised Dalpatram's ability to compose impromptu poetry to Raghuram Shastri Dante. The shastri composed the first line of a verse, '*Surat maan surat kar surat kamini saathe* (In Surat, try to enchant the enchantress)', which Durgaram wrote down for Dalpatram to complete. Dalpatram immediately

Kavi—I was somewhat in awe of him, I will admit, but I had never approached him, nor did I have any great desire to do so. He would recite *garbi*s and *lavani*s about the evils of intoxicants at the Parejgar Mandli[*] near Fort, but I had never attended any of those events. I had, however, attended his reading of *Hunnarkhan* at the library in 1907. I was standing at some distance and heard it, but returned home immediately without waiting to approach him. I revelled in the headiness

---

said, '*Pad poorvardh lakhyun chhe Durgaram haathe* (Half the verse is written by the hand of Durgaram).' The shastri understood that Dalpatram was quick-witted but not a poet who could compose on the spot. The second incident: a puja was being conducted at a Mahadev temple near Durgaram Mehtaji's house, and Tapishankar Gandhrap asked Dalpatram to explain something about Nayika *bhed*. He found Dalpatram's reply quite unsatisfactory. Durgaram had also told me that Dalpatram couldn't identify ragas well. Once, during the puja of *chaudas* (fourteenth day of the month), this even became a topic of mirth. That Dalpatram couldn't identify ragas is true. Once, in Ahmedabad, when I had recited verses, he tried to name the ragas. The knowledgeable ones there had smiled inwardly at his lack of knowledge. Those who were in the audience and know their ragas will remember this incident.

[*] This mandli published a periodical, *Parhejgaar*, which was mostly written by Bhai Mahipatram Roopram.

of my youth and didn't really care deeply about many issues.

That same year, I landed up at a reading by Manmohandas Ranchhoddas—a recitation of a speech in verse form. As the organizer was about to acknowledge and honour him for his recitation, Dalpatram Kavi stood up to sing Bhoja Bhagat's verses, thus drawing the attention of the audience to himself. After this, Manmohandas did not receive any honorable mention, which would have been ordinarily due to him. I remember this incident today and remember having written a dohra about this in *Rasapravesh*:

The young man with a tap to the head, the boy–
poet's rise did he shun
Inwardly much did the youth burn, a disfavour to
poetry was done.

Viram 6

1854–56

1. When I went to Bombay in January, my father had already made arrangements for my employment. Accordingly, from 10 January to 10 June, I taught English to Dwarkadas, the son of Jivraj Baluvala, from 11 a.m. to 4 p.m. every day, for which I received a salary of Rs 25. That boy had little interest in learning. In those five hours, he would get up ten times for a break. His memory was poor and so was the effort he put into his studies. Since he was an undeserving student, I felt I was wasting my time. Further, I did not think it correct to keep taking a salary, and so I quit.

2. From early morning till about 9, I used to learn the *Siddhantkaumudi* from a Marathi shastri. I did this for a few months until I reached the *apatyadhikar* section and then I stopped.

3. About a month after reaching Bombay, I began to suffer from severe physical discomfort. This was perhaps due to the heat of the intoxicants ingested in Surat (I had stopped taking intoxicants in Bombay) as well as the lack of conjugality.

4. In those five months, my mental condition went somewhat like this: on the one hand, I wanted to achieve fame through knowledge and learning, perhaps study law and appear for the bar exams, or enjoy the pomp of being a Mamlatdar (not a *munsif*); perhaps I would learn many languages, such as Sanskrit, Persian, English, Urdu, Hindi, Marathi, and become a linguist like Sir William Jones; perhaps I would attend college, become financially independent by teaching English and spend time in the pursuit of knowledge.

    On the other hand, after going to Bombay, I began to feel that certain things that I had indulged in during my days in Surat were sinful, and I was filled with remorse. I would ask my father, in the guise of helping another person, how, if one's behaviour was sinful, could one be saved from punishment and so on. He said that some actions were sinful in the eyes of the world, but true repentance was the key to achieving a release from sins. I was troubled by being away from many loved ones in Surat after arriving in Bombay. In such a condition, what would be the point of earning money or fame or even living? Such thoughts of disaffection from the world overwhelmed me. In this mental state, I had even proposed to my father that since we were both widowers, why should we be trapped in the web of worldly possessions? We should retire to some village and live on the banks of some river or lake, eke out a simple living through labour and immerse ourselves in learning and the pursuit of knowledge. What pain he must have suffered at seeing my condition. Since I was his only and much loved son, he never said a harsh word to me. What could he do? He himself enjoyed the good things of life but was thwarted by his lack of money and conjugality. To top it all, he had to listen to my rants. But all credit to him that in such moments, all he did was to quell my doubts by citing from the shastras and worldly instances. Oh, my dear father, how I miss you today! Pradyumnaji Hirachandji, a senior member of my caste, would be able to bear witness to my mental state in those days.

5. Once, in this turbulent state of mind, I was sitting in the Native Book Club, a library situated in the building of the General Assembly Institution. I saw a fair young man in a Gujarati turban arranging books. Later that day (I don't remember how), we got talking, despite being strangers. That was Zaverilal Umiyashankar, a fellow caste member who was attending college. It was he who inspired me to begin going to college. My father, too, was supportive of the idea. On 10 June, I paid Rs 60 and enrolled myself as a paying student in the Clare Scholar's class. Two months after this, I had to go to Surat to conduct the death anniversary rites of my wife. While in Surat, my uncle died on Bhadarva Vad 5 of 1910 and I had to extend my stay for a further period. Thus, I ended up spending two months in Surat. On my return, I resumed my studies, and after burning much midnight oil, appeared for my exams in December. I obtained 60 per cent marks and became a West Scholar—I began to receive Rs 15 every month.

6. At that time, our professor of accounts was Dadabhai Naoroji. I do not recollect who the other professors were and what subjects they taught. Some of the students who had appeared for the examinations with

me complained to Dadabhai that the grading system was unfair, and that since my attendance was not as regular as theirs, my marks should be reduced to some extent. Dadabhai replied that unlike them, I had not made a single spelling mistake in my answers. I was quite proud that despite my not having read a single English book during my three-year stay in Surat, I had got all my spellings right.

7. In 1855, I was still in an anxious state of mind—I was rendered restless by my thoughts. I sought escape in idle conversation and dreams of going abroad. While others worked at their lessons, I would remain lost in my thoughts, often neglecting to pay attention to the professors' lectures in class. For this, I was given the nickname 'Lalaji' by my companions Murlidhar Girdhar (who is today in the court of Kachchh), Zaverilal Umiyashankar (who is a businessman today) and Tribhuvandas Dwarkadas (who is presently with Kamruddin Taiyyabji Vakil's office). By and large, I neglected my lessons and assignments, but when Harkness taught Falconer's poem 'The Shipwreck' or Wordsworth's poetry, I paid close attention. The descriptions of the beauty of nature moved me deeply.

To this day, I remember the valour and stoicism of the sailors in 'The Shipwreck'. I also remember that in August, I had written about a hundred lines in English on some topic and showed it to Mr Reid, who had simply laughed at the attempt.

8. I tried to control my restlessness but was not successful. In September, I came across some verses by Dheero Bhagat and was obsessed by them. The verses were in keeping with my renunciatory frame of mind. On the fourth or fifth day, it occurred to me that I should compose something along those lines—and I wrote '*parbrahm jagat karta re smaroni bhai har ghadi* (dwell upon His name, bhai, every moment, He who created the universe),' and the next day I wrote, '*jeev tu murakh samje re kahu chhun ghela fari fari* (O mind, fool that you are, not to understand the Truth, I say this again and again).' It then occurred to me that if I composed verses of my own, it would perhaps help my mind to be more stable. I wanted to achieve peace of mind in any manner possible, so I decided that I would keep myself busy composing verses since it had a cathartic effect on me. I also thought that after all, education, earning money and fame, having a wife etc. were all means to

achieving happiness. If composing poetry gave me happiness, then that was what I should pursue. I would somehow manage to eke out a living. In that manner, at the onset of my twenty-third year, I began composing poetry—I do not quite remember when I composed my first poem, but my birthday occurs sometime during that period; I decided to attribute the date of composition of my first poem to my birthday and have since kept count of my days of writing poetry from that day—Bhadarva Sud 10 of Samvat 1911, or 21 September 1855.

9. From then onwards, every morning I would write one verse on prayer or learning and would go to college at 11 a.m.

10. I appeared for my examinations in December. I should have secured 60 per cent, but due to my aforementioned disturbed state of mind, I could manage only 50 per cent. Thus, I couldn't be a Second Normal Scholar.

11. In the monsoon of 1854, I enrolled myself in the Buddhivardhak Sabha and read out an essay on avoiding adultery and prostitutes. I had also read out my poems on the benefits of learning history and the disadvantages of indulging in intoxicants—I have lost

the first of those poems. I had not composed those poems following the rules of prosody but had tried to follow the style of Samaldas' *chopai-chhappa* that I had read. I also tried to follow the style of poetry in the books of Kavi Dalpatram and Manmohandas. At that time, in Bombay, people had no notion of poetry, and the name of Kavi Dalpatram was known to but a few. My so-called recitation was appreciated by the members of the Buddhivardhak Sabha and this encouraged me greatly. I was a bit like a figure among ciphers.

12. I felt that the members of the Buddhivardhak Sabha did not quite understand the intricacies of poetry and poetics, and although I could keep on presenting my poetry to them, it would not be good for me. It was necessary that I learnt the grammar of verse as early as possible; why, I did not even know the rules of composing a dohra or a chopai. At around this time, in October 1855, I read in *Buddhiprakash* that the science of composing verse was called *pingalshastra* (prosody). I began to look for books on prosody in Sanskrit–Prakrit, but couldn't find any in Bombay.

13. I considered writing to Kavi Dalpatram, but wondered if he would casually brush aside my request. Perhaps

he might not be willing to provide an honest response. I remembered his behaviour during Manmohandas's lecture in 1851. I abandoned the idea of writing to him, at least for the moment.

14. In January 1856, I mentioned my search for books on prosody to an acquaintance, Tuljaram, a Bhargava Brahmin from Surat who was residing in Bombay. He gave me Kalidas's *Shrutbodh*. But who would teach me? After much searching, I found a Nashakkar Shastri, Dadadev. He was rather uncaring, but I managed to find time between my college hours and would take lessons from him. In about eighteen days, I had a good understanding of the *Shrutbodh*. While I was learning *Shrutbodh*, I was simultaneously applying its rules in Gujarati. From that book, I managed to understand and compose in many metrical forms, but I could not find the rules regarding dohra and chopai, since those metres did not exist in Sanskrit.

15. Manmohandas had published books for women composing verse, aphorisms that preached morality. I realized that he must have access to some work on Indian prosody. I wrote a letter to him as below:

Blessings of Narmadashankar, son of Lalshankar, to his most valuable friend and poet Manmohandas, son of Ranchhoddas.

I am enclosing herewith a piece of writing (poems from an essay about shunning immoral behaviour), requesting you to critique it. I would request you to provide annotations of poetic scansions, correcting any mistakes and providing the names of the metres employed. The manuscript may please be returned to me at the Elphinstone Institution. I would be greatly obliged if you do so.

I plead ignorance on the subject of poetry; I have a deep desire to learn and am confident that I will be able to do so. I earnestly hope that you will be willing to hold my hand as I embark on this pilgrimage into the realms of prosody.

I have written much else besides what I have submitted to you with this letter. Much of it has been written approximating your style and that of Dalpatram.

It is said in English that 'poets are born', one needs intellectual ability to write poetry. Mere knowledge of the rules of prosody is not sufficient in my opinion—just as only intellectual content is not sufficient. It is necessary to clothe those thoughts in appropriate metrical language—clothing is primary, adornment secondary.

> Without salt, no food has taste
> A *kirtan*, sung in a proper raga, can make an
> atheist devout
> (This too may be corrected)

I can improve my intellectual ability and reasoning but without appropriate technique, it will be an incomplete improvement. Doubts will consume much time. I need to study works on prosody in Prakrit.

It is not possible to gain knowledge without a teacher. In this matter, I am not unlike many *kanbis* of Surat who have never studied poetry and poetics. I am hence filled with apprehension. I do not have anyone else who can teach me. I therefore pray that if you take on the task of being my teacher, I promise to do you justice by being a diligent and dedicated student. I may be forgiven for having taken so much of your time.

Please convey my regards to Bhai Mohanlal and respected Ranchhoddasji.

I will be in Surat in April for my wedding, and I hope to see you and gain some knowledge from you at that time. For the moment, I would appreciate it if you could recommend some introductory books on prosody. What more should I write? Please do not hesitate to demand any work from me.

16 February 1856

(I did not receive a reply to this letter. When I decided to write my story [*Mari Hakikat*], I requested Manmohandas to send me the letter if he had it. After several months, he sent me the letter, and I have provided its contents here.)

16. Since I did not receive a reply from Manmohandas, I stopped writing poetry using the *matra* metre. I continued writing poetry that employed the *akshar* metre as well some *padas*.

17. In April 1856, I came to Surat, and in May, on Vaishakh Sud 15, Samvat 1912, I married Dahigauri,* daughter of Tripuranand Pandya, and returned to Bombay.

---

* I had no intention of remarrying after the death of my first wife. My father arranged my betrothal with someone, but this did not meet with

18. After the wedding, on returning to Bombay, I found myself feeling increasingly uninterested in pursuing education at the college. The reasons were many—my increasing passion to write poetry, my ambition to gain accolades as a writer in Gujarati, Sanskrit and English, the desire to cease financial dependence on my father and the fear of financial insecurity that would inevitably follow. It seemed that eventually, I would have to

the approval of several of our relatives, and the matter became a topic of discussion at all meetings and functions of the caste. I did not like this. One day, in a burst of anger, I demanded from my in-laws-to-be that they should return my horoscope. I received a reply that it was destroyed. I broke off the engagement. This was highly uncommon among the caste of Nagars, since there was a shortage of eligible girls. How much must my gesture have pained my father? For me to unilaterally go back on a commitment that he had made! Only my father would have tolerated such behaviour! I was concerned about my father; I had smashed his hopes of seeing me start a family. Eventually, fresh inquiries were resumed. On Kartik Sud 3 of Samvat 1911, my betrothal was finalized once again, and as mentioned above, the marriage was solemnized in the Vaishakh of Samvat 1912. I had expressed my reluctance to sit on a horse during the wedding procession, but my father insisted, and I finally relented and rode a small, black horse. Similarly, I did not want to invite the entire community for the wedding feast, but only a select few. But here, too, I had to give in.

abandon college education since the First Normal Scholarship was available to only three candidates, and given my attitude, I wasn't hopeful of getting it. My thoughts flitted from those of financial independence to attaining release after death. I also realized that my instability had led to my wasting time. My father advised me to take up a regular job and confine the pursuit of poetry, Sanskrit or whatever else to my spare time. I was also swayed by the thought that since there was no material on prosody available in Bombay, I would have to go to Gujarat. For all of these reasons, I decide to quit college, and on 28 June 1856, I submitted my letter of resignation saying that I was being offered a private job (this was only an excuse). On 19 August, I left college after taking a certificate from Mr Harkness:

This is to certify that Narmadashankar Lalshankar was admitted into the English School of the Elphinstone Institution in January 1845; that he continued to attend regularly till April 1850, when he obtained the Clare Scholarship; that he left the college shortly afterwards and returned as a paying student in June 1854; that in December following he obtained West Scholarship and regularly attended the Second Year class in which he made a creditable appearance having obtained 50 per cent marks at the Scholarship Examination; that he possesses fair abilities and would in my opinion have taken a pretty high place if he had continued to prosecute his studies. His conduct so far as it has come under my observation has been uniformly good.

Bombay, Elp's Ins'n   (Signed) JOHN HARKNESS, LL.D.

19th Aug. 1856   Principal

19. While I was still studying in college, the Ra of Kachchh* had written to Harkess requesting him to recommend someone for the position of a school teacher at a salary of Rs 100. Harkness recommended myself and Murlidhar to the Ra, providing all details of our caste and conduct. He particularly recommended me insofar as teaching was concerned, given my experience as a

---

* I had expressed interest in going to Kachchh in the hope that I would be able to locate books on prosody in Indian languages among the many books in the Royal Library. I had also hoped that one day, if the Ra became fond of poetry, my importance would increase, and I would be able to pursue my interest freely.

school teacher. However, the Ra selected Murlidhar, who was a *kanbi*. At that time, there was a tacit policy not to employ Nagars in the darbar of Kachchh.

20. I served as the editor of *Buddhivardhak Granth* from March to December 1856, except for a two–three month break. Towards the end of that period, after leaving college, I applied to the registrar of the Sudder Court, Mr Cokeson, for the post of the Gujarati deputy head clerk, but nothing came of it.

21. After leaving college, I stayed at home writing poetry and simultaneously learning the *Vrittaratnakar* and *Raghuvamsha* from Devshankar Shukla. I managed to complete my study of the *Vrittaratnakar* but could manage to complete the study of only the second and third cantos of the *Raghuvamsha*.

22. On 15 August, an announcement was published in the *Rast Goftar* inviting essays on the origins and history of the Gosai Maharajs. The prize was Rs 100. I decided to try my hand at it and got in touch with Vaijnath Shastri, an acquaintance of mine, who was a disciple of Jeevanlalji Maharaj of the main temple in Bombay.

I requested him to lend me books on the Maharajs, but he regretted his inability to take books out from the temple. He also informed me that I would be able to find useful books on the subject in Surat. I informed my father that I needed to go to Surat to access some material. The idea was that even if I couldn't find books on this subject, I would be able to search for material on Indian prosody. I arrived in Surat in November. Unfortunately, I couldn't locate much material on the Vallabhacharya sect, and so I dropped my efforts towards this end.[*]

23. Here in Surat, I contacted my friend Jaduram, who in 1851 used to publish *Gyansagar*. I told him that he had to somehow manage to locate a book on Hindustani prosody. We made a lot of effort to that end and, in the course of our efforts, landed up at the home of Gordhan, a mason.[**] I recited for him some of the padas that I had

---

[*] I had, much later, written the essay and kept it with me, but I have no idea where it is now.

[**] This mason was an expert in both painting and stone carving. His calligraphy was excellent. He had also read extensively works on the Vedant written in Hindustani. He is currently in charge of the

written. He was quite impressed and said that his guru, Laldas, was an excellent poet, and he, Gordhan, had in his possession all the books of Laldas. He asked us to come the next day if we wanted to browse through them. I went to his house the next day, and he opened a large chest which contained a book: *Chhand Ratnavali*. He said that he could not allow me to take the book home, but I was welcome to copy it at his home. Every morning, I would go to his home with paper, quill and ink, and would make copies. He also showed me some beautifully painted and well-written works of pictorial poetry, also executed by Laldas. I was tempted to make copies of these also.

I told Gordhandas, who was called Bhagatji by others, that since there were constant discussions on intellectual and spiritual matters going on in his home, it was difficult for me to concentrate on making copies. I told him that I would appreciate it if I were allowed to take a few pages home every day, where I could make copies. I would return them in

---

construction of my new house. It is rare to come across such craftsmen. There is none comparable to him in Surat today.

a day and take fresh pages the next day. He agreed. I would take a couple of the pictorial poems and hand them over to an artist to make copies of the illustrations. I would go home, have supper and later in the night, collect them. I would then inscribe the poetry in the illustrations. In this manner, I managed to make copies of all the pictorial poems and a copy of the *Ratnavali* as well. I managed to understand the contents of the book on account of my knowledge of Sanskrit. This book proved invaluable in my understanding of the rules of various metrical forms of poetry such as dohra and chopai.

24. After 15 December, I went to Bombay and was to take up a job teaching an officer of a regiment. But he insisted that I would be hired only if I had a certificate of reference from Vinayak Vasudev. I went to Vinayakrao and requested that he should examine me and issue a certificate. Vinayakrao said, 'Surely you are making fun of me, Narmadashankar!' He issued an official certificate as under:

Bombay, 22 December 1856

Certified that Narmadashankar Lalshankar is qualified
to teach Guzerathee.

(Signed) VENAYAK WASUDEV
Oriental Trans. to Government.

I taught that Britisher for a few days, but since some
work came up for him, he had to stop.

Viram 7

1857–59

1. In January, I was attempting to put forth my thoughts on educated versus uneducated men and women in a poem. At that time, my father came across an article on prosody in the 1855–56 issue of *Buddhhiprakash* written by Kavi Dalpatram. On seeing this, he said that it was quite an achievement to write about prosody in the form of metrical poetry. I replied that it was nothing noteworthy. He said that he would accept my statement if I could compose a similar metrical stanza. I stopped what I was doing and began to compose a mnemonic stanza. My first line was, 'la-la-gu makes the *sagana* cluster, the *jagana* cluster is la-gu-la.' My attempt at encapsulating a prosodic principle in verse pleased him and he said that I had proven my ability. The

couplet I had composed conveyed the rule that two short syllables (*laghu*) followed by a long one (*guru*) formed the sagana group of letters. I had created the word 'lalagu' to make this pithy and poetic.

2. In February, I assumed the post of a teacher in Gokaldas Tejpal School at a salary of Rs. 25. At that time, Tribhuvandas Dwarkadas was also appointed at the same salary, but he resigned shortly afterwards. I would stay on after school hours, gazing at the sea, the sky and the boats, and in this solitude, I began writing the verses that became the basis of my *Pingalpravesh*.

3. In March, I completed writing my essays on 'Women and Guru'. I had the *Pingalpravesh* scribed by my father and had it printed on the litho press. It was presented to the general public on 6 April.

4. Bhai Mahipatram wrote a review of this edition of *Pingalpravesh* in *Satyaprakash*:

> The *Pingal* that we were all awaiting is now published. We have received a copy through the grace of its publisher Kavi Narmadashankar Lalshankar. On reading it, it is apparent that it is

a mature work and of much use. Its able writer has now joined the annals of our great poets.

There hasn't been a single work in Gujarati that addresses the rules of prosody. This gap has been filled by bhai Narmadashankar . . .

The *Rast Goftar* of 19 April said: 'There was dire need of such a book and that need has been met. The author has not only explained the rules of poetry but has also composed illustrative examples. This clearly demonstrates that he himself is a poet of no small standing.'

In the June 1857 issue of *Buddhiprakash*, Kavi Dalpatram wrote: 'There was not a single work in Gujarati that explained the rules of poetry. Such a book has now been prepared and published by bhai Narmadashankar . . . A great deal of labour must have gone into preparing such a book, the first of its kind in the Gujarati language . . .'

5. In the period before my *Pingal* was published, Kavi Dalpatram had written a series of articles between October 1855 and October 1856 in *Buddhiprakash* on the rules of prosody. But they addressed *vrittas* (metres) of up to sixteen matras only. There was no reference to

Aksharvrittas, syllabic verse, and the dohra metre was also not addressed.

6. After publishing *Pingalpravesh*, I started studying *Chandralok*, a treatise on the fundamentals of figures of speech (*alankar*), and *Nrisinhchampu* from Devshankar Shukla, and by the end of December, I had completed my study.

7. My salary at the Gokaldas Tejpal Vidyalaya was increased to Rs. 35. But I felt that a job in a government school offered higher status and better prospects. I therefore applied on 26 January 1858 to Mr Smith for the post of assistant master in the Elphinstone Institution Central School.

8. One 3 February, I received a positive response from them. On 7 February, I resigned from the Gokaldas Tejpal School and on 8 February, joined as assistant master in the Central School at a salary of Rs. 40.

9. I began writing *Alankarpravesh* in January. I also began the study of Rasaprakaran (chapter on rasas) from the treatise *Prataprudra* from one Maharashtrian named Farasram.

10. I published the poetry that I had written over the period from September 1855 to March 1858 in two compilations—*Narmakavita* Vol. 1 on 18 April and *Narmakavita* Vol. 2 on 14 May 1858. I also published my works *Alankarpravesh** on 25 April and *Rasapravesh* in June** or July.

---

* I had planned to print the *Alankarpravesh*, like the *Pingalpravesh*, on the litho press. I had gone to visit Dr Bhau to inform him that I intended to dedicate the book to him, not in the hope of getting any monetary help but because he was one of those who would truly appreciate rasa alankar. He, on his own, suggested that I should get it printed on typeset and that he would bear the cost of printing. I did so, but the doctor delayed the payment so much that I ended up paying the printing cost. I did not feel comfortable approaching Dr Bhau for the money, but my father insisted that there was no harm since Dr Bhau himself had offered to pay. It bothered me. Someone who intended to pay would have done so immediately. Why should I have to go to him again and again and demean myself and waste my time? But I gave in to my father's insistence and approached Bhau several times. Often, he would not be available, and he made promises a couple of times. After several months, he paid an amount of Rs 125. I seem to remember that it was about Rs 25 more than the actual bill.

** I estimate this period based on my application for the copyright of *Rasapravesh* on 23 July.

11. In 1858, I became the secretary of the Buddhivardhak
    Sabha and the editor of *Buddhivardhak Granth*. We had
    announced in the *Buddhivardhak Granth* that contributions
    submitted and selected would be paid an amount of one-
    fourth of a rupee per page. After this announcement, the
    Ahmedabad agent of the *Buddhivardhak Granth* wrote
    thus to us on 15 May and 10 July:

> Kavi Dalpatram composes garbis to be published
> by the periodical *Streebodh* and is paid an amount
> of rupees 0-4-0 per line by them. If you wish to
> publish his garbis etcetera in your periodical, I can
> approach Kavi Dalpatram with a proposal. Do let
> me know at the earliest without fail.
>
> If, for your periodical *Buddhivardhak*, someone
> composes and submits poetry in Gujarati of a very
> high order, then a garbi has the same number of
> metrical lines as a dohra. The periodical *Streebodh*
> offers four annas for a metrical line. If your
> association pays the same amount, I will submit the
> poems. If you do not find them worth publishing
> and you return them, there would be no monetary
> obligations on either side. Only if you find the

poetry as good as or perhaps better than the works of great Gujarati poets such as Vallabh Bhatt, Premanand and Samal Bhatt, you may decide to publish it, or else it may be returned. Please seek the opinion of your association and reply to this letter at your earliest convenience, for which we will be grateful.

In reply to these, I wrote on 20 June: 'The announcement has been published at the personal instance of the editor in order to encourage young men. The editor is not agreeable to paying the rates as paid by *Streebodh*. As far as poetry is concerned, 100 metrical lines may not be worth one-fourth of a rupee while a single metrical line may be rewarded with Rs. 25. The editors do not wish to publish the sort of garbis that are currently published in *Streebodh*. However, we will pay, just as we do for prose, the rate of one-fourth of a rupee per page for poetry. If someone like Kavi Dalpatram does a favour by sending his poetry, not just the editors but the entire association will accept the same with respect and a deep sense of obligation.'

On 24 July, Lallubhai wrote: 'Kavi Dalpatram has sent a *garba* of seventy-two stanzas for publication in your periodical. If the editors and the association find it worthy of publishing, they may do so. The poet does not make a claim of any specific monetary value—only that if you like it, publish it, otherwise you may decide not to pay anything. If the association does not approve of it, it may be sent to us by return post. As to your response to the worth of a stanza, I have conveyed it to the author of the letter.'

That *garba* on the joy of an educated daughter was published in the *Buddhivardhak Granth* in the same year and Dalpatram was paid Rs. 1.5 for the five pages, which he accepted.

12. With my increasing affinity towards poetry, I found the daily drudgery of dealing with the schoolchildren loathsome. I showed my poem 'From ten thirty to five does the babbling continue . . .' from *Rasapravesh* to my friend, the assistant school master. He agreed completely with the sentiments expressed. Since I felt increasingly alienated from my tasks in the school, I,

without informing my father, tendered my resignation on 23 November.

13. Mr Smith issued to me a certificate as under:

> Elphinstone Instin. Central School
> Bombay Novr. 23rd 1858

I have much pleasure in testifying to the satisfactory manner in which Narmadda (Shankar) Lalshankar discharged his duties as assistant master in the Central School.

His knowledge of Gujarati rendered his services particularly valuable and it is with regret that I part with him—of late he had undertaken the instruction of the Candidate Class in that Branch and displayed a great zeal and ability.

E. I. Central School   (Signed) W'm HENRY SMITH
Head master

14. I came home and with tearful eyes, looked at my pen and said, 'Henceforth, I seek refuge in your lap.' Since

I had made no financial arrangements for my future, my father was quite angry with me, but all he said was, 'Bhai, what was the need for such haste?' I had thought that since I had an affinity towards poetry and towards matters moral and spiritual, and further, since no other occupation seemed to give me satisfaction, I should become a Hardas, one who recites Harikatha or religious narratives. Not only would this provide a source of income, it would allow me to continue my engagement with learning. In any case, I had a gift for language, and there was a dearth of a Hardas who could deliver religious discourses in Gujarati. My command over the language was strong and with a deeper study of Sanskrit, I could write *akhyaans* (narrative poems) in Gujarati and earn a living. Having taken this decision, I approached some Hindu merchants for financial help that would allow me to pursue my learning of Sanskrit and simultaneously prepare myself to deliver such discourses. One of them gave Rs. 250 and another gave Rs. 50. One refused to give me anything and even mocked my ambitions. I was disappointed at getting an amount far below my expectations but did not lose heart and decided to pursue the path that I had selected.

15. During this period, at the request of a friend, I translated into verse the *Laghuhitopadesa* and submitted it for publication. It was subsequently published in my absence (I was in Pune at the time).

16. I went to Pune in early December. I began my study of *Laghu Kaumudi* and the play *Vikramorvashya* under Neelkanth Shastri and Vishnu Shastri, respectively. I completed the study of the play, as also two commentaries of the *Laghu Kaumudi*. Balashastridev, an expert in grammar and poetics, used to teach about fifteen students at his home. I would note down a few prefatory slokas from the *Kavyachampu* and would analyse them from the perspective of poetics. What was poetry?* What was great poetry? What was the difference between alankar and rasa? I would go to him with such questions, and he in turn would provide answers with relevant and definitive citations from various texts. From him, I refined my understanding of prosody, alankar and rasa. In addition, I studied

---

* I wasn't sure what I was writing was proper poetry. But my study with Balashastri reassured me that what I was writing was indeed proper poetry.

a famous Jain commentary[*] on the *Vritta Ratnakar*. It contains detailed descriptions of the spread of Aryaa Geeti and its forms.[**] At night, I would read the *Lingapurana* and the *Adhyatmaramayana*. All of this took me about four months (my previous study of Sanskrit stood me in good stead here). With all this, I managed to write and send to Bombay two essays, 'Vishayi Guru'[***] and 'Guru Ni Satta' (The Authority of the Teacher).

---

[*] I had, at Bhau Daji's request, given him my copy of this text, an old and venerable text in the Western Matrika.

[**] Once, in 1859, at the home of Mathurdas Nathubhai, I asked Kavi Dalpatram if he was familiar with the forms of Arya Geeti. He replied in the negative.

[***] Mathurdas Lavji had expressed his interest in publishing these essays and offered me Rs 75. I had expected that they would be printed by litho press. During that period, Bhagwandas Purushottamdas organized an exhibition by girls. On the train on the way to the exhibition (we were travelling together), Bhau Daji expressed his desire to get a thousand copies of each essay printed on type at his expense. I had not suggested this but he proposed this since he personally preferred 'type' and also since this would ensure wider circulation. I followed his instructions, and the bill arrived. But then neither of them reimbursed the expense. Reader, just imagine the consternation and worry that this caused to this writer. I have had many such experiences. I borrowed money to

17. I was staying with my wife's uncle. I did not find this arrangement convenient, and he did not like the idea of my staying elsewhere on my own. So I decided to go to Bombay and return to Pune after making alternative arrangements for my accommodation in advance. I went to Bombay on 20 March 1859.

18. It was clear that I would live my life independently in the pursuit of knowledge, but I was also looking for some source of livelihood. I had tried to make provisions till such time as I could achieve the competence to be a Hardas, but I could raise only a meagre Rs 300. Ever since I had quit my job at the school, I was determined that I would not seek any financial aid from my father—I was in no position to do so. On my return to Bombay from Pune, I heard of a potential patron— one Harishankar of Chudaranpur, a devout follower

---

pay the bills and distributed the essays free of cost at the temple. Where would I keep so many copies in my small, rented room? My father and Mathurdas insisted that I should persist and remind Bhau and I did so for some time but finally gave up sending reminders. After about six months, some Bhatias sent me Rs 100, an amount much less than the printing cost. Due to my own financial precarity and at the instance of my father, I accepted this amount.

of the Swaminarayan sect. He had served earlier as an assistant teacher in a government school under Raosaheb Bhogilal. Hence, I assumed that he would be a young man about my age and that we would get along well. If he helped me, both the reformists and the traditionalists would have no cause to complain due to Harishankar's role. I would earn my living while being able to pursue my study of poetry, religious narratives as well as Sanskrit. I decided to meet him. Someone told me that Chudaranpur was only about 20 gau (80 miles) from Bhavnagar. This was an added incentive, since I had always wanted to visit a princely state. I even wondered if Bhavnagar would be as grand as Bombay!

19. I came to Surat and from there, with a young relative, set out for Ghogha by way of Bhagva Dandi. We first went from Rander to Kundiyana. I still remember how, after eating a somewhat undercooked khichdi prepared by my companion, we drank in the natural beauty on the outskirts of the village by a well; how, after bathing, we ran joyfully barefoot, our bodies still dripping, uncaring of the thorns piercing our feet! We reached Bhagva Dandi—at 10 in the night we attempted to

reach the boat trudging through the muddy beach, but the mud was so deep that we couldn't reach the boat and spent the night on the beach, shivering in the cold. We spent the next morning on the boat gazing at the shore, and at about noon, the boat set off. We reached Ghogha next morning. At the Hatkeshwar dharamshala, a Nagar lady inquired if we were there on some government-related work.[*] I said no, and I still remember with amusement the look of disapproval on her face. We hired a carriage to Bhavnagar, where we were hosted by Pran Narayan, a fellow caste member and a master at the local English school. On inquiring, we found that Harishankar had fallen out of favour and was actually in jail. Besides, Chudaranpur turned out to be 200–220 miles from Bhavnagar! Everyone advised us against travelling in the heat, and I too decided to cancel the plan to go to Chudaranpur. I had, after all, come without informing my father and he would worry if the trip lasted too long. I stayed for four days in Bhavnagar. Several people came to meet me, of which

---

[*] This instance makes it amply clear how much respect people had for the representatives of the government. Even a lowly clerk commanded more respect than a merchant or a pundit.

some (from my caste) were from the side opposing the administration. I heard their stories. I moved around the town. Bhavnagar was a disappointment—a village compared to Bombay, despite being the capital of a prominent princely state! The administrator of the court, who happened to belong to my caste, invited me to dinner. I was in a fix. I hated attending dinners where I did not know the host well, which is why I don't attend our caste dinners—there is just so much small talk and nonsense, a complete waste of time. For me, a good dinner engagement means sitting with friends and having an intelligent and interesting conversation that covers a range of topics.

Worried about offending a senior person and yet reluctant to go, I tried to think of various excuses to wriggle out of this engagement but finally accepted the invitation on the advice of Prannarayan. I had met Gagabhai, the host, once earlier. As a host, he seemed to lack warmth. His behaviour towards me was somewhat patronizing, but he did come across as a mature and perspicacious person. Then his son Vajalbhai took me to his room. That young man really treated me well and with respect. I was offered tea and paan-supari. He seemed to be quite in favour of social reforms. He described to me with great passion the hard work he was putting in at the school for girls that he had established. I felt that he was a generous person, hungry for friendship and for acknowledgement of his work. He seemed to be committed to the cause of social reform. After dinner, Gagabhai talked to me about the dyke he had had constructed and the roads that he had had repaired—as if to convey that he took his responsibility to construct and maintain public works quite seriously. The conversation turned to the study of Sanskrit. I suggested that the state should invite shastris and have the many texts there translated into Gujarati and publish them. I do not think the idea appealed to him since he did not respond. He then showed me the works of Manoharswami and expressed his interest in having them published at his expense.[*]

---

[*] These padas were in the Balabodh script and were written in Gujarati as well as in Hindustani. I had my clerk segregate them and selected those I thought were worth publishing. I had them printed at my expense. I wrote requesting that a *hundi* should be sent for the printing expense of Rs 300 (approximately, I can't remember the exact amount) so that I could pay the printer. I would sell them at a reasonable cost and claim the profit as my remuneration. I requested an early response so that the title page may be finalized, and I also sent a set of the

That evening, Vajalbhai and Chhaganlal took me to the dyke. We went to a community hall of the Vohras. We sat there, had paan-supari and listened to some singing by a singer named Shivram. Vajalbhai seemed to be a simple person, but Chhaganlal seemed to be a man of the world—quite good-looking, fond of the good things in life, including poetry and music. He was sweet-tongued and seemed to get around. His face had an expression of smug satisfaction when he made Shivram sing some poetry that he had written. As the evening advanced and the lamps were lit, we headed to the palace. There was a group assembled on the terrace of the palace. I saw a dark-skinned man seated on the parapet. Thinking he was an attendant, I headed in his direction to seat myself there. Just then, Samaldas

---

printed manuscript. I received a reply that there were many errors in the printed version, to which I responded that it was not unusual in the first edition. Any errors would be corrected in the second edition. From their response, I gathered that they were not satisfied with my effort, and so I paid the printer from my own pocket. I fixed the price at Rs 2 and put my name as the publisher on the title page. Later, I received Rs 300, which I did not want to accept, but I succumbed to my father's insistence. However, I sent off all the books to Mehervanji Bhavanagari, instructing that they be sent to Bhavnagar.

addressed him—it was the king himself: 'Maharaj, this is Narmadashankar the poet.' Frightened out of my wits, I somehow managed to bow and pay my respects and requested him to visit Bombay. The king just smiled and said that he had been planning to do so. I sat with the others for some time and after paying my respects to the king once again, I came home.*

---

* During the five minutes that I was with the king, I had looked at his face for barely a minute (out of a misplaced sense of shame, a fear of being misunderstood and of being in breach of protocol), but I got a sense that the king was a simple man, of ordinary intelligence and of serious temperament. But I also sensed that there was a streak of wickedness about him. That night, I went to a Muslim courtesan's place with an acquaintance of mine to listen to her singing. She had had a falling out with the court. It seems that the court expected her to perform there on her own initiative, whereas she felt that a formal invitation should be sent to her—only then would she perform. However, some of the ordinary citizens of the town would go to her place to hear her. There were only a handful in the group there who were connoisseurs. The rest were just merchants who came to escape the daily grind of their day. They offered a few rupees and left after a while. Finally, there were about ten of us left. There was a Muslim spectator who made frequent requests for various ragas. The lady was irritated but conceded. He then asked her to perform the *kerbo*, a special dance. The lady said that she hadn't performed the *kerbo* since a long time and wasn't sure if she would be able to do justice. The man

The next day, when I departed for Surat, Gagabhai gave me a shawl and a turban (worth about Rs. 30) as a farewell present. I was reluctant to accept such gifts but he insisted.* I reached Ghogha, where Jayantilal, Narbheshankar Vakil, Jamiatram Munsif and others came to see me off as I boarded the boat to Surat.

20. When I was in Bombay, I had a keen desire to visit various princely states. My visit to Bhavnagar cooled this desire somewhat. However, I reasoned that Vadodara

---

insisted, and finally she let loose her hair and performed the *kerbo*—it was quite good. He then asked her to play the sitar. That courtesan was known to be an accomplished player of the sitar, sarangi and dholak. It was about four in the morning but by then, she was also in form and she picked up the sitar. I remember being entranced by her beauty at that time. The soft light cast by the two lamps placed before her, her fair face, loosened tresses, her nimble fingers flying over the strings of the sitar, her left foot keeping beat, the sight of her waist as her body swayed with the notes that filled the air, faint drops of perspiration on her fair forehead and her intoxicating eyes—every moment of that scene is vivid even today. I have preserved the memory of that incident in the two lines of my *Rituvarnan*: '. . . with loosened tresses, beating time with her foot, she plays the sitar . . .'

* On reaching Bombay, I sent books worth about Rs 25 to Vajalbhai, Chhaganlal and some others as gifts.

was closer, was the capital city of the Gaekwads and therefore must be worth seeing. It should be visited at least once—if I didn't like it, I needn't go there again. Besides, I would probably be able to go to Dabhoi and get access to the padas of Dayaram. The memories of that visit are encapsulated in the last ten lines of my poem 'Vadnu Jhaad' (The Banyan Tree). I visited Vadodara and had my fill of it. I could not visit Dabhoi as Dayaram's disciple, who would have given me access to Dayaram's padas, was himself in Vadodara to read the *Okhaharan* during the month of Chaitra. I have mentioned the contents of my conversation with him in a note in the beginning of the section on Dayaram in my *Narmagadya*. While I was in Vadodara, I was struck by the realization that I was merely wasting my time in my travels to Bhavnagar and Vadodara. I was not doing any constructive work. I composed 'Dukh Harta Sukh Karta' in Vadodara. During my stay, I never visited the court even once—by that time, I had lost interest in viewing displays of pomp and grandeur. My mind was on my work. I had seen the king only once, and that too from some distance, while he was viewing a wrestling match.

21. I travelled in all for twenty days. On 19 April, I replied
to two letters that I had received. The first was dated
22 March and was from W.H. Newnham, assistant to
the Director of Public Instruction. It was a request to
translate the glossary provided in Arnold's *Hitopadesha*.
I replied that I would send it in a few days. I was
busy during that period, and I had my father carry
out the translation. Since I didn't receive any further
communication regarding the matter, I never sent the
translation. I learnt subsequently that the published
version was translated by Ranchhodbhai Uderam.
Perhaps it was because I did not send the translation to
the government or perhaps Ranchhodbhai was asked
to translate at the recommendation of Mr Hope.

The second letter was dated 31 March and was
from E.I. Howard:

I request you will do me the favour of becoming a
member of the vernacular class book committee for
the purpose of settling once and for all the standard of
Gujarati orthography.

I replied to the effect that 'I am extremely grateful to
you. I have since long wanted to express my thoughts

on this matter and I have keenly felt the need for the existence of a committee of the sort that has been set up under your leadership. I sincerely hope that the committee will continue to be in communication with me regarding this subject.'

22. After returning to Bombay at the end of April, I was planning to go to Pune to continue my training to be a Hardas when I heard that Dalpatram Kavi would be arriving in Bombay. My friends teased me that I was running away from Bombay to avoid him. I cancelled my plan to go to Pune. On 27 May 1859, Kavi Dalpatram came to Bombay with Deputy Inspector Bhai Mohanlal to get medical treatment for an eye ailment.[*]

23. On the day of his arrival, or the next day, I was at Vasudev Babaji Navrange's bookshop near Mumbadevi

---

[*] In 1858, Mangaldas Nathubhai had written a letter to Kavi Dalpatram inviting him to Bombay. The Kavi had set the condition that Rs 100 or so, his travel cost, should be borne by the inviters. A fund was started for this, and Mangaldas and others from the Buddhivardhak Sabha had contributed. I myself had contributed Rs 2 to this fund. Then, for some reason, the trip was cancelled. Mr Hope was to spend the monsoon of 1859 in Bombay. Perhaps the Kavi thought it advisable to ensure that his trip coincided with that of his mentor.

Chowki when Dalpatram arrived there. He asked me where Babaji's bookshop was, and I said that this was the place. He went upstairs to meet Vasudev Babaji. Vasudev Babaji informed him that Kavi Narmadashankar was also present, indicating towards me. Dalpatram had not been acquainted with me during my days in Surat. We embraced. He said, 'I heard of your visit when I went to Bhavnagar. I delivered a lecture on Vijaykshama and the king was so impressed, he wanted to give me a large reward. I said that he should instead donate Rs. 10,000* towards setting up a collection of books and manuscripts, and the king agreed.' So saying, he rose to leave. He turned back

---

* At that time, I had a very high opinion of Kavi Dalpatram, since he had been writing poetry for such a long time and he had presented his poetry at various princely courts. But this statement left me stunned. I was convinced that I could never come up to his standards. Later, I came to know that no such temple to knowledge was ever set up and that he had been given a reward of some 200–300 rupees. On my trip to Bhavnagar, he had commented, 'Yes, of course, he had gone to Bhavnagar in the hope of being awarded a royal annuity—fat chance!' If I remember correctly, it was the then editor of *Samsherbahadur* who told me this. I had also retorted at that time, 'Of course, Dalpatbhai would say that. After all, I don't have a Forbes who can divert funds from the royal treasury and grant me an annuity.'

and said to me, 'I am staying at the Swaminarayan temple. Why don't you come tomorrow and take me to meet Dr Bhau?' I agreed and went to him the next day. He was memorizing some piece that he had written in praise of Dr Bhau. He asked my opinion, 'Do you think this is all right?' I said, 'It is very good.' I took him to Dr Bhau's place and, after introducing them, left for home.

24. On 13 June, Bhai Karsandas Mulji delivered a lecture on Pravahi Shastra (one of the paths in the Pushtimarga tradition) at the Buddhivardhak Sabha. At the end of the lecture, Kavi Dalpatram, in praise of the Buddhivardhak Sabha, recited some shlokas composed in the Naaraach metre. Hearing him, I was impressed with Kavi Dalpatram's poetry. This was the first time that I had, with some attention, heard the poet reciting his own poetry.

25. On 17 June, I was sitting at Vasudev Babaji's bookshop when Gangadas Kishordas turned to me and said, 'You will find out tomorrow.' I asked him, 'What will I find out?' He just chuckled and repeated, 'You will find out tomorrow.' Gangadas was referring to what

he considered would be a competition between me and Kavi Dalpatram the next day. I, on the other hand, thought that he was referring to the publications that we had made against the Maharaj and that we would be receiving a notice of libel for the same. I said, 'Luther had said that even if my enemies are equal to the number of tiles on the roof of the palace, I shall not change my stand. But I say, if those tiles were to break into multiple fragments and even if the number of my enemies is more than the number of those fragments, I will not change my stand as regards the Maharaj.'

26. The next day, Saturday, 18 June, Gangadas called me to his school and said, 'Vinayakrao has sent a note and instructed you to take your best poems and go to Bhagvandas' bungalow in Walkeshvar.' I said, 'I will certainly go, but to listen, not to recite.' I went home determined that I would never recite my poetry in the presence of Dalpatram. It wouldn't matter if my poetry was not very good, but if my poetry was superior to that of Dalpatram, it would embarrass him and that would be inappropriate. It didn't matter what the spectators wanted. After all, what did they care? At 5 p.m., I left

for the venue without a single poem with me. On the way, I met a friend who offered me some paak, which I ate. I met Dalpatram and Gangadas on the way and we went together to Walkeshvar.

The group met at 6 p.m. There were no Parsis present in the group, it was mostly Vaniya merchants. Bhagvandas said to me, 'Let Dalpatram recite his poetry and then you recite yours.' I said, 'No, that will not happen. I am just as keen to listen to Dalpatrambhai as all of you. In any case, you have heard me several times.' I said to Dalpatrambhai, 'Please go ahead.' He began with two poems in Hindustani. He then recited the poem where the names of Mr Hope and Dolatrai were woven into the poem like an acrostic.* Then, Dalpatbhai, accompanied by his nephew, began to sing the Yadavasthali.** And as he was completing his

---

* Dalpatrambhai invariably recites this poem along with 'I, the young son, slept in cradle' and letters of Ram-Sita—to demonstrate his cleverness with words. I believe that if you take into account all his recitations at various places—Bombay, Surat, Ahmedabad etc.—he must have recited this poem at least 200 times. A fine poem!

** This must have greatly disappointed the gathering, which had come with very different expectations of Dalpatram. At this stage, I felt really sorry for Dalpatram. Hadn't he even considered what would appeal to

recitation, Vinayakrao announced, 'Now we will hear a poet from Bombay.' I said, 'Not today, please—you have heard enough from me on previous occasions.' The vaniyas were impatient since it was supper time for them, so Varjivandas,* who was anyway a bit upset with me, said, 'Let it be some other time—it is getting late.' But Vinayakrao was adamant that they not leave without listening to a poet from Bombay. I was in a dilemma. For one, I would be breaking my resolution. Secondly, I had eaten paak just before coming here and that would affect my voice. I hadn't even brought any of my poems with me. Vinayakrao insisted that I should recite whichever of my poems I remembered well. Left with no choice, I got up. I decided to recite the dohra and *malini* relating to the nine rasas from *Rasapravesh* since I had them almost by heart. I stood next to Dalpatrambhai and said, 'Dalpatrambhai is like

---

the audience—his first in Bombay? To recite the Yadavasthali, which extols the evils of intoxication, in front of an audience sitting with hookahs by their side! Besides, he recited the dohras and chopais like a semi-literate man sitting on a riverbank reading Samalbhat's poetry to himself. No wonder the audience was bored.

* I had, at the instance of Mangaldas, written a poem entitled 'Vrijjeevan Tu Prerna Kar', which had upset Varjivandas.

an ocean—with a vast treasure of poetry that he has written over the years. Compared to him, I am like a puddle, a novice at writing poetry. Dalpatram has been composing poetry for twenty years, this is merely my fourth year—I do not have anything that can compare to his work, but since Vinayakrao is so insistent, I will present something.' Despite my voice being short of its best since I had consumed paak, I recited the dohra–malini with clear enunciation. The topic being novel and the singing good, the audience was spellbound. While I was singing, Vinayakrao, who was standing by my side, his hand on my shoulder, exclaimed in admiration, 'Wah! Wah, Narmadashankar!' Although I was concentrating on my recitation, I could see that Dalpatram was feeling diminished. This bothered me and every time Vinayakrao began his exclamations of praise, I would press his boot with my foot—to indicate that he should refrain from expressing his praise aloud. Finally, everyone got up and headed over to where refreshments were served, and we (Dalpatrambhai and I) sat down to eat the Alphonso mangoes that were being served. I tried to make up for any neglect that Dalpatrambhai might have felt by carrying on an enthusiastic conversation with him.

I have referred to this incident in the 24 June issue of
Samsherbahadur.

27. That this incident created an adverse impression on
Dalpatrambhai became clear the next day when he
was talking to the editor of *Samsherbahadur*. On the
topic of the essays written on the Maharaj, he said,
'Lallubhai, he is intelligent and writes good essays.
When he reaches my age, he will be able to write good
poetry too.'

28. Bhau had sent for me and told me that he would start
a fund for me and Dalpatram, so I should continue
writing poetry. I cancelled my plans for Pune with the
hope that I would get some part of this fund and that
would allow me to pursue the reading and writing of
poetry. There would be no immediate need to train as
a Hardas and earn my living; it could be done later.
I was fearful that Dalpatrambhai had been writing for
twenty years and would have a vast collection* of poems,

---

* I became aware of Dalpatrambhai's ouvre much later—he had mostly
preferred to read his old, published works and a significant part of
that oeuvre were garbis. I had once asked him, 'How much of your
writing—whether regarding the Swaminarayan sect or other works—

whereas I had very little. I grasped every opportunity that presented itself to write new poems.

29. On 5 July, I read my 'Essay on Unity' at the Buddhivardhak Sabha; on the 11th I read the poems 'Lalita' and 'Saahasdesai'; on 28 July, at Dr Bhau's home, I read my praise to God at the resolution of the revolution; on 7 August, after Dr Bhau's address at the girl's school run by Mangaldas, I read out a garbi; and on 21 November, I read a poem on independence in the Buddhivardhak Sabha.

30. I published the fourth, fifth, sixth, seventh and eighth volumes of *Narmakavita*. A Parsi friend, Dadi Kharsedji Ghogha, gave Rs. 100 to defray the cost of publishing the fifth and sixth volumes.

31. Many of the Gujarati speakers of Bombay of the time had no understanding of poetry. However, from 1857 onwards, they began to get some exposure to rasas and alankars and there was an increased interest in

---

remains unpublished?' To which he had replied, 'About as much as has been published.'

poetry. With the arrival of Kavi Dalpatram, due to our recitations, discussions, critiques in the press and so on, the popularity of poetry increased manifold. The Parsis in particular took to it with particular fervour. Dalpatram was invited to read his poetry at various places, and he accepted honorariums whenever they were offered. I, on the other hand, never accepted any money. On the contrary, I would often spend from my own pocket to meet my conveyance expenses. In those days, neither Dalpatram nor I had a free moment. Whenever Dalpatram chose to recite a long poem, he would memorize it the previous night (he did this so that he would not have to read and strain his eyes).

32. It so happened that the Buddhivardhak Sabha planned to raise a fund for Dalpatram—to honour him by commissioning a statue or establishing a scholarship in his honour. When I heard this, I was quite indignant. It was foolish, I thought, to confer such honour on a poet while he was still alive. One of my friends noticed my indignation and wrote a longish article in the *Samsher*, making references to Dr Bhau, Gangadas Kishordas and others. On account of the article, the idea of the statue and scholarship was dropped. I had

nothing to do with the article. But Dalpatrambhai somehow felt that I had instigated that article as well as others in the press that compared our poetry, which seemed to opine that 'Dalpatram's poetry is ordinary while Narmadashankar's is erudite'. I plead complete innocence in the matter. I admit that it bothered me when I saw Dalpatram getting more praise than he deserved. Dalpatram was extremely upset when he saw his poetry being labelled ordinary. He mentioned before a Parsi friend of mine, 'Just see the how the newspapers write such appalling things about me.'

33. Dr Bhau called me and said, 'The issue of the fund has been put to rest. But Dalpatram is our guest, after all, so let him be the beneficiary of all monetary help.' I consented, but I was a bit peeved with Bhau.

34. I had rented a room in the Laad Ni Wadi for my writing. Dalpatram was also staying nearby. So we ended up meeting quite frequently. Some of our conversations were as below.

I asked him, 'In poetry, should the rules of *hrisva* and *deergha* and the purity of Sanskrit words be maintained?' He replied, 'No, that would make writing poetry in Gujarati impossible.'

'Have you carried out any study of the *Rasalankar*?' He said, 'No, I have only studied pingal, prosody in some depth.' He had mentioned this to my father also.

When I asked him, 'What according to you is the best poetry?' he replied, 'Bhai, it takes ten years to be said to have entered the realm of poetry. The best poetry is that which, when sung, appeals not just to the Gujarati but to speakers of other languages also.' He then went on to recite, *'Tane roki rahi Radhika rang jaamyo ghano rasiya, rajani rahij thodi* (Radhika restrains you, O rasiya! Resplendent is the moment and receding the night) . . .' I queried, 'Why is this an example of good poetry? Is it merely because of the alliterative effect of the "r" sound?' He countered, 'That in itself is no mean achievement.' Later, when Dalpatram was not present, I said to my clerk, Narbheram, 'Bhai, do you understand where the poetry lies in this instance? The poetic element here is that of the lover's impatient pleading and the beloved's reluctance to let go. That is what makes it good poetry, not the alliterative use of "r". It is the underlying, deeper meaning that gives poetry meaning. Dalpatram's example was not inappropriate, but his own understanding was limited.'

When my father read the chhappa 'Ganga girija
dvesh klesh nit teno thaaye (Ganga and Parvati, rivals are
they eternal)' from the Samplaxmi, he praised it. I had
said at the time that it was probably not his original
idea. Subsequently, I did come across a shloka which
had a similar meaning. I had actually asked Dalpatram
about this chhappa, 'Were these your own thoughts
or were they inspired from writings in Sanskrit?' At
first, he was silent. I then continued, 'There is a shloka
in Sanskrit which expresses a similar idea.' He then
said, 'Yes, I had composed that chhappa based on the
Sanskrit shloka.'

I had asked him, 'Please tell me how and when you
were first attracted to poetry.' He had replied thus:
'I had studied the Sama Veda in my childhood—I have
read the dasha granthas but I do not have them by
heart. In childhood, I fell into bad company. I used to
go with my maternal uncle to Muli village. There was
a swami, Bhoomanand Swami, who was originally
a potter by birth. I would often visit him with my
uncle. My father was hopeful that I would become a
follower of the Swaminarayan path and come to my
senses. Once, a learned monk, an Acharyaji, came
to Muli. He said, "If this boy wants to learn poetry,

he should—he will excel at it." I said, "But I need to meet my material needs in the meantime." The Acharyaji said, "We will take care of your boarding and lodging—go to Ahmedabad and learn." There was another, Vishnu Brahmachari, who was told to go to Kachchh and learn there. I came to Ahmedabad, where I began to read various books on language that the monks had written. I also began to learn the *Saraswat*, but it could not sustain my interest—my mind was completely obsessed with poetry. Life was tough there. Many a time, we would not be given our provisions on time.'

I had invited Dalpatrambhai to my home for dinner—I had fed him basundi and poori.* After dinner, I had gifted him *Prataprudra*, a Sanskrit volume on rasa and alankar. I had said sincerely, 'Dalpatrambhai, our views on poetry may be very different, but that should

---

* When the newspapers began writing articles critical of Dalpatram's poetry, he, believing me to be the instigator, had turned against me. It saddens me to say that I had, with all my heart, wished for us to be friends and had invited him to dinner in my home. Despite this, Dalpatrambhai had said to someone while boarding the steamer (if he denies it, I am willing to take an oath with God as my witness), 'Damn his basundi-poori.'

not diminish our affection for each other.' He had said, 'Not at all. After all, see how the Punch (Parsi Punch) has placed our hair knots in each other's hands.' I said, 'Why should it matter what the press writes? The Punch is only after a bit of fun. Believe me if you can, that despite our divergent views on poetry, I consider you as an equal and have great affection for you.'

35. A party was held to honour Dalpatrambhai in Walkeshvar. At the end, everyone delivered speeches in his praise, I too among them. I had said, 'Dalpatrambhai was a pioneer in composing poetry on the subject of social reform. He is the last of the composers of traditional poetry and the first to compose modern poetry. The progress of a nation depends on the progress of its women. Dalpatrambhai's endeavours to compose poetry for the women and for their progress are of particular value etc. etc.'

36. In the same year I, with the help of some of my friends from Kachchh who were proficient in Hindustani, achieved familiarity with the Hindustani works *Chintamani Pingal*, *Sundarshringar*, *Bhashabhushan* and *Rasikpriya*.

37. From 1859 onwards, I freed myself from blind religious beliefs and became a cultural reformer.

38. It was a practice among the sub-group of Bhikshuks in our community that during community meals, the women would remove their upper garment and would sit to eat with a single cloth wrapped around them. I took the initiative to put a stop to this practice, starting with our home and with the support of Dolatram Vakil and Gulabnarayan, two cousins of my mother. This was during the annual feast of Hatkeshvar in April 1859. On that occasion, only five women had dared to break this tradition. Today, every woman of the community sits at the feasts wearing silk blouses. At that time, many women got up from the feast at this sacrilege; the Brahmins were angered, but no one dared to say anything. I chose this issue because on one occasion, the women of Grihastha and Bhikshuk groups were sitting down to a community meal in the open plot in front of my house. The Grihastha women were wearing their blouses, whereas the Bhikshuk women had removed theirs. I saw this from the window of my house and the thought plagued me: when the women of two groups within the same community could sit

together for a community meal, why should one group have to remove their upper garment? If the concern was pollution, then surely since they were sitting together, both should follow the same practice. If the Grihastha women could wear their blouses, why not the Bhikshuk women? Were the Bhikshuk women servants or slaves of the Grihastha women? In any case, it did not behove women of an upper caste to sit in the open without their upper garment.

Viram 8

1860

1. In January 1860, Bhai Mahipatram was preparing for his travel to England. In the meanwhile, Hiralal Umiyashankar got an article on Bhai Mahipatram published in the *Samsherbahadur* in the absence of its editor. The article claimed that the Nagar community had granted permission to him to travel abroad. That issue fell into the hands of Sheth Bhagvandas Parshottamdas. He had mocked the Nagar community in front of his clerk, Dahyabhai, who, by the way, shared his residence with Hiralal. Angered at the mockery, Dahyabhai gave Hiralal a dressing down. He threatened Hiralal that unless he apologized and publicly withdrew that article, his engagement would be annulled, and he would be cast out from the Nagar community. I do not know if he actually published

a withdrawal, but he did offer penance by lighting a ghee lamp at the temple of Lord Mahadev. The Nagars of Bombay prepared a document that every member signed. When this document was presented to my father for his signature, he said, 'My son is not present at the moment. We will do the needful on his return.' I was, at that time, enjoying myself at Chimod in the company of my friends Nanabhai Rustomji, Ardeshar Faramji and others. On my return, those seeking our signatures came back and we, father and son, said to them, 'We cannot bring ourselves to sign this document.' Bhai Zaverilal had also made a similar statement. Due to this, seven of us were separated from Bombay's Nagar community. I brought out a handbill of appeal (see *Narmagadya*, page 423). After a fairly long time, some of our friends intervened and we were allowed back into the community and permitted to attend the community meals.

I must clarify here that many feel that I was among those who encouraged Bhai Mahipatram to travel to England. The fact is that I became aware of his plans of travel only when the last resolution was passed and he proceeded to Bombay. Never has Bhai Mahipatram sought my opinion or advice by way of a letter.

2. On 7 July 1860, I came out with 'Tattvashodhak Sabha' (see *Narmagadya*, page 434). But prior to that, I had published *Narmakavita* Vols. 9 and 10, and in August, I published *Dayaramkrut Kavyasangrah*, a collection of Dayaram's poetry.

3. In July, I got published four lectures that were delivered at my home (two on Bhakti and two on Saakaar). In the same year, I delivered a lecture on Sajeevaropan-Rupalankar in the Buddhivardhak Sabha and one on remarriage (5 October) in the town hall.

4. The incident with Jadunathji went somewhat like this: when Jadunathji came to Bombay, he had mentioned to Lallubhai Gopaldas, the deputy clerk of the Sudder Court, 'It would be good if Narmadashankar could visit me.' One day, I went to visit him at Byculla—he didn't know me, nor did I know him. I entered his room as he was preparing to leave. He, on hearing that a Vaishnav wished to see him, went back and seated himself on the couch. I went up to him, folded my hands respectfully and said, 'I am the same Narmadashankar that you wished to meet.' I was about to seat myself beside him on the couch, but it occurred to me that it may not be appropriate. I sat on the floor next to the

couch. I inquired of him if he planned to spend the Chaturmas in Bombay. He replied in the affirmative. We made some small talk that I do not recollect, but finally I said, 'It seems that you were about to leave to go somewhere. I will come whenever you ask me to.' Both of us then got up.

In July, Jadunathji visited Mangaldas's girls' school and said that he strongly encouraged the education of girls. He thus said what no Maharaj before him had said. The reformists, therefore, were convinced that Jadunathji was a good person. It seems that in a private conversation with Lakhmidas Khimji, on being asked what he thought of remarriage, Jadunathji had said that there was nothing objectionable about it. Lakhmidas Khimji and others told me to write positively about him, but I thought that until I met Jadunathji in person and gleaned his innermost thoughts about social reform, I should not write anything in his praise. However, I did concede to compose some impromptu verse that praised him.

One day, I went to visit him in the temple. After some perfunctory exchange, he said, 'Come in the afternoon, we will talk.' Dhirajram and I went to meet him later that afternoon. The Maharaj was resting on the couch. I requested one of the attendants to inform the Maharaj that Narmadashankar had arrived. Despite our presence, the Maharaj stretched himself and said, 'Tell him to come later.' Those words pierced me and I was furious.

Eventually, the reformists began to understand that the Maharaj presented a different side of himself in their presence but was completely different with the orthodox Vaishnavs. He was also quite angry with me for my essays on the Maharajs and openly criticized me. My essay on Bhakti had further angered him. That was how our relationship became adversarial.

Then, on 15 August, I printed a handbill. For details of the handbill and the related footnote, please see *Narmagadya* Vol. 1, page 424. Based on the handbill, it was decided to have a meeting and hold a debate (see *Narmagadya* Vol. 1, pages 426–27).

I have written an account of the meeting in the *Satyaprakash* of 26 August. In addition, I would like to say this: none of the reformists accompanied me, and I went there at about 3 p.m. Jadunath and I had not planned to debate the issue of remarriage then, but we wanted to prepare the outline of the debate. So we spent our time in discussion without specifically addressing this issue. At about 8 in the night, I said, 'It is quite late, so let us wind up this discussion—we will debate the issue of remarriage at length some other time.' Before this conversation, I read aloud quite passionately the exchange of correspondence that had occurred between us before this meeting. I also said during the meeting, 'I would not even share the stage with a religious leader who plays fast and loose with the truth, let alone conduct a debate with him. It is only to prevent people from saying that the reformists have lost that I am here.' When I began reading the letters, Jadunathji said, 'You may publish them if you like; do not read them aloud here.' I said that it was necessary that the letters be read aloud to the audience present there. While I was reading them, Jadunathji sat with lowered eyes, clearly ashamed. When the meeting ended, a mischief-mongering Pokarna Brahmin stood up and shouted, 'Down with Narmadashankar!' There were about 200 Vaishnavs in the hall and about 800 more in the compound outside. Many of those had plans to thrash me. There was no police bandobast. Just then, my father, who had no idea that his son was in the meeting, arrived and approached me, alarm writ large on his face. I was worried that the old man would be crushed if there was a stampede. I arranged for him to leave with my friend Kisandas Bawa. I turned to Jadunathji and said, 'If anyone so much as raises his hand on me, know that you will be held responsible. So tell the crowd to disperse.' I got up to leave but couldn't find my shoes. I quickly descended the stairs with only my socks on. Some people in the compound asked me, 'Where is that fellow?' To which I simply said, 'There he goes.' As soon as I exited the compound on to the road, I borrowed a pair of shoes from a friend and managed to reach home. Soon, there was a small crowd outside my home, shouting and cursing at me. But I was safe in my home, behind locked doors. Another Maharaj and some of the shastris present at the meeting were impressed with my oratorial skills. One of them, Vishnushastri, from somewhere in north India, actually arrived at my home the next day. He was teaching the Maharaj Sanskrit but became a close friend of mine. He praised my poetry and was absolutely in awe of my *Rukminiharan*.

5. Although the reformists had not accompanied me to the meeting out of fear, they began to criticize me. They said that I should not have raised the issue of

the origins of the scriptures. I replied, 'I will not say something that I do not believe in. Had the debate on remarriage taken place, I would have proved, basing my arguments on Jadunathji's contention that "the scriptures have a divine origin", that remarriage is acceptable. You all can rest easy.'

The notion that the scriptures were not divinely ordained was debated extensively in the press. As a part of this debate, an article was published in the *Satyaprakash* on 21 October alleging some immoral behaviour on the part of Jadunathji. Based on this article, Jadunathji filed a suit of libel on 14 May 1861. The matter proceeded for some time and finally the hearings began on 26 January 1862 and lasted for forty days (see 'The Maharaj Libel Case').

6. The students in schools found it difficult to understand some of the words in my poems. I had planned to prepare a vocabulary comprising the difficult words from these poems and providing their meanings. In the process of doing this, I realized that there were many such words. This inspired me to prepare a full-fledged dictionary that would include most words in the language. Dr Dhirajram supported the idea, and

on 18 November 1860, I started work on compiling a
dictionary.

7.   While the subject of remarriage was a topic of extensive
     debate, a couple willing to undergo remarriage came
     forward. A Brahmin woman named Diwali, on the way
     to Nashik, made a halt in Bombay. There, she put up at
     a Vaniya's home. This gentleman was known to me and
     came to me: 'The topic of remarriage seems to be a hot
     topic nowadays. If you come to my home, I will introduce
     you to a woman who is willing to remarry.' I went over to
     meet her, and she said, 'I am willing to remarry. But if we
     face any difficulties on account of this, the reformists have
     to stand by us and help us.' I said, 'Not only will you live a
     good life after remarriage, you would also have set a good
     example for other women. In such a case, who wouldn't
     stand by you?' I left after the conversation and was
     thinking about placing this proposal to my friends. The
     next day, when I visited Dr Dhirajram, I saw our Gujarati
     friends along with the Brahmin woman and that Vaniya
     acquaintance there. I watched in surprise at the discussion
     that my friends and that Brahmin woman were having.
     Finally, we came to the conclusion that the woman was
     firm in her resolve. Now, the task was to find a suitable

man. That Vaniya, with help from his group, located a Brahmin named Ganpat, who seemed to be a suitable person. They spent almost eight days in Mahalaxmi together, and on the ninth day, some friends and I met him at Vasudev Babaji's shop, where we questioned him: 'Are you doing this for the money? Will you abandon her and ruin her life? Are you really doing this to set an example for society?' He replied, 'The reformists will gain credit for this example that I am setting. I will perhaps be ostracized by most members of society. If, after remarriage, I abandon her, where will I go? I am not doing this for the money.' His responses, as well as the fact that he and the woman had had eight days to get acquainted and evaluate one another, gave the reformists confidence to proceed. Their marriage was conducted as per rituals by a Brahmin at Dr Atmaram's home. Many members of the Paramhans Sabha and the Buddhivardhak Sabha were present to offer their congratulations to the couple (see *Satyaprakash*, 16 December 1860).

Shortly after this marriage took place, Jadunathji Maharaj decided to exact his revenge on the reformists. He sent his acolytes to Ganpat, who tried to influence him by saying that the reformists had laid a trap for him. If he agreed to go against them, he would be accepted back into the community. They even managed to get him to agree to sign an agreement in the office of a British lawyer. The agreement stated that he was under the influence of *bhang* and was not in his right senses when he remarried. Further, he was misled by the reformists and so-and-so reformer had offered him money and now they had gone back on their promise etc. As luck would have it, a person who was in favour of the reformists happened to be present in the lawyer's office. He advised Ganpat to take a day and think things over before he signed the agreement. Ganpat too began to have doubts. What if he signed and the Maharaj went back on his word? Where would he be then? He did not sign the document. He narrated some of this to me that night. I, on behalf of the reformists, spent considerable time assuring him of our support. Much later, on another occasion, he became inebriated and began to curse the reformists, particularly me. Many wealthy individuals had aided his cause. As a result of his behaviour, they, along with many of the reformers, now began to disassociate themselves from him.

Ganpat and Diwali began to pester me and Balaji Pandurang by coming to our homes. We had wished them well and done them a favour. They, on the other hand, used foul language and denounced our actions.

Despite this, whenever they were in dire financial straits, we took pity on them and helped them as much as we could. When that woman died as a result of an illness, I gave a fair sum of money. Her last rites, however, were delayed on account of many factors. The reformists had already dissociated themselves and therefore did not turn up. I had, in the past, tired of their harassment, lodged a formal complaint with the police and so could not be present for the last rites. I did provide substantial financial help, though.

The first attempt at remarriage did not have a such a positive outcome. The only consolation for us reformists was that at least that couple could spend some time in each other's company and provide emotional support to one another. It was another matter that later, they chose to ruin their lives by turning against the reformers—no doubt, the Maharaj's machinations had something to do with it. First-time experiments are invariably like this. People say that the first example of remarriage should have been an exemplary one, but such a thing is well-nigh impossible. The reforms that have occurred are a result of actions of ordinary persons and often even those of foolish ones.

8. That very year, I was invited by a Marathi intellectual to join a religious society that strived to break the caste system. I said, 'If the members pass a resolution that each of them will act as ambassadors, addressing public meetings all over and declaring their intentions and beliefs and act in accordance with them, I would be more than willing to join.' He said, 'All that can be taken care of later. For the moment, we want you to join us.' At his insistence, I joined.[*]

9. That year, my Dahigauri, at the age of thirteen, began to live with me.

---

[*] The period from 1860–61 was the period during which my passion for social reform was at an all-time high. My conviction was that any effort of reform done on the quiet was cheating God and the public. So whatever one did should be done openly. One such incident occurred when there were differences among the members during a meeting, and six of the members decided that they would openly support reform. I was among them. I said to my father, 'This is how it is, so if you want to dissociate yourself from me, please do so.' He was alarmed (on many occasions, I had, through my passion for reform, hurt my father but always told him, 'Bhai, I will not be dishonest with you. If this hurts you now, so be it'). Ultimately, since five of those members backed out, I too had to exercise restraint. Otherwise, I would have gone public long ago.

Viram 9

1861–64

1. On 3 May 1861, that is, Magh Vad 7 Samvat 1917, my childhood friend Parbhuram died in my home in Surat. The death of this long-time companion, an icon of probity and fairness, affected me deeply.

2. In early April, I established intimate relations with two cultured women.

3. On 13 April, Bhai Mahipatram returned to Bombay from his travels abroad. I went to the port to receive him. It had been decided that he would stay at the home of Dhirajlal Vakil, and so he proceeded there on arrival.

4. Ever since Mahipatram's departure, the next president of the Buddhivardhak Sabha, Gangadas* Kishoredas, had been insistent that I should take the initiative and dine with him as proof of my convictions since the Nagars were a notoriously crafty people. I would explain that my dining with him would not ensure his acceptance by the Nagar community. Both of us would be excommunicated. If the Nagar friends who had written in support of Mahipatram were willing to dine with him, I would be happy to join. Since the goal of the reformists was to break the caste barrier, why shouldn't we all dine together? I had already made up my mind that I did not mind being excommunicated and would dine with any caste after that. That determination and Gangadas's constant goading finally led to my writing a handbill titled 'Akashvani' on 15 May, and I distributed it to the group at Dr Bhau's home, where everyone had gathered to meet Mahipatram (for 'Akashvani', see *Narmagadya*, page 429).

---

* When Bhai Karsandas Mulji returned from his travels abroad and it was time for Gangadas to dine together with him, he developed cold feet and finally backed out! Talk about the pot calling the kettle black.

Once, Mr. Howard inquired through my friend Balaji Pandurang, 'Narmadashankar, why don't you help Mahipatram?' I responded saying, 'I am willing to offer all the possible help and as far as dining together is concerned, if four others volunteer, I will be the fifth to join.'

5. In those years, by the good grace of my student Ganpatram Hemji, I used to teach poetry recitation at the Zoroastrian Girls' School* at a salary of Rs 25. Twice a week, I offered tuitions in the Gujarati language to two businessmen, Mr Sterns and Mr Hobart, for which I was paid Rs 50. I also taught a couple of wealthy Parsi gentlemen.

6. In that year or the next (I can't quite recollect), I presented a religious discourse at Goculdas Tejpal's bungalow in Walkeshwar, for which he gave me Rs 50.

7. I also learnt music for one hour every day.

---

* I worked here for two years and one month—from 1 December 1860 to 31 December 1862.

8. In that year, I published *Kavi Kavita* Vol. 3 and *Narmakosh* Vol. 1. This was in addition to several poems that I wrote but did not publish.

9. From the beginning of 1862 till about June of that year, I worked day and night with my friends Nanabhai Rustomji and Ardeshar Faramji towards compiling an English–Gujarati dictionary. My one-third share of the profits derived from its sale was quite substantial.

10. In February, I made my deposition as a witness in the Maharaj libel case.

11. From May onwards, I suffered from the pangs of separation and wrote several poems to express my anguish.

12. In that year, I published *Narmakavita* Vol. 1 (a compilation of seven years of my poetry).

13. I toured the Deccan and Gujarat in the period between 10 September and 9 October. I have, in the second volume of *Narmakavita*, incorporated my impressions of this tour in a poem called 'Pravas Varnan'. I found myself deriving immense pleasure from nature's beauty during

this tour. Ordinary features, such as the lush green grass of the forest, the mud of the riverbank, the pebbles on the beach, affected me greatly. It was almost as if I was in a state of spiritual bliss. This trip was physically demanding and on two occasions, life-threateningly perilous, but I was undaunted. My obsessive need to revel in the beauty of creation somehow rejuvenated my weakened body. Roaming among the mountains, wandering in the wilderness or losing my way in the dark—all these gave me pleasure. During my trip to the Deccan, I was accompanied by my clerk Zinaram, while on my trip to Gujarat, my companions were my friend Parbhuram Mehtaji and my senior clerk Narbheram.

14. In December, I published the second volume of *Narmakosh*.

15. I had once, while talking with my friend Karsandas Madhavdas, expressed my desire to spread the message of social reform to each and every village in Gujarat. A mission would be set up in Bombay and on its behalf, I would make public orations. It would mean hiring a shastri and setting up an establishment for writing and publishing, which would probably cost about Rs

300 per month (this would include my own expenses). I had asked him if he would contribute this amount, to which he said that he would contribute Rs 100 every month. I said that there was one more person willing to donate a monthly amount of Rs 100 but that still left me one donor short. However, nothing further came of this matter.

16. I received a demand for tax surcharge on 28 January 1863 for the year 1862–63. I was staying in Mazagaon at the time. I was upset that despite my solemn declaration, aspersions were being cast on the honesty of a public figure such as myself. I remained in a state of anxiety for about four days. On 3 February, I decided, against the advice of my assessor friends, to go in person to the commissioner of income tax, Mr. Curtis, who was known for his short temper. They were convinced that I would be arrested. I entered his chamber and said to him, without concealing my agitation, 'These are my financial statements and this is my reputation. If you still demand the additional surcharge, I will pay it, but my actions in public are a reflection of my principles.' He was angry but, seeing my indignation, simply said, 'Save this speech

for your home.' However, the surcharge amount was finally reduced.

17. I had begun publishing issues of *Narmakavita* Vol. 2 from the beginning of 1863, and by the end of the year, brought out the entire compilation as a single volume.

18. In that year, I was distressed due to financial strain, a broken heart and estrangement with some of my friends. The frenzy in shares had led to people making windfall profits, which further exacerbated my sense of anguish— how unfair it was that people who made sincere efforts in honest endeavours were not rewarded, while those who adopted dishonest means were reaping all the benefits! I distracted myself by taking recourse to writing—lyrical works, Shanta Rasa to calm my mind and Vira Rasa to give me courage to take on this unfair world.

19. In the period from 1862 to 1863, I sought refuge in reading the biographies of English poets and their poetry as a way of coping with my mental distress.

20. On 16 November, Kartik Sud 5, I invited my friends to my home and made my students sing my poems with musical accompaniment.

21. Towards the end of that year, my father was bedridden in Surat and I had to make several trips to Surat from Bombay. My last visit was in January 1864, and on the third day after my arrival, 18 January, he achieved eternal release. During my father's illness, Narbheram had attended to him with great diligence since I had been mostly in Bombay.

22. In Bombay, along with the craze for the share market, there was a craze for theatre. Theatre companies that had no clue what good theatre entailed somehow put up shows that made the public laugh, which enabled them to reap the moolah and flourish. Two Parsis approached me with a request to allow them to use my poetry in their plays. 'People do not have the capacity to understand and enjoy my poetry,' I replied. When they insisted, I put forth my condition, 'I will charge Rs 100 per session. You will bear all the costs of the singers, musicians and the rental charges of the theatre. In turn, you can keep all the amount from the ticket sales.' The performances of the Narmageet Gayak Mandli took place between 6 and 16 May. The response from the public was lukewarm, and the organizers suffered a

loss. The mandli was disbanded. Out of pity for the organizers, I returned their Rs 200.

23. Then I went to Ahmedabad, where Mr. Curtis told me, 'The people here are keen to hear you speak. Please deliver a lecture before leaving.' I said that since I had pressing engagements and had to leave, it would be possible only if the talk could be arranged at short notice. He said, 'Premabhai is not here.' I responded, 'The lecture is for the people. How does Premabhai's presence or absence matter?' He said, 'I will inform Dalpatram.' Subsequently, when I met Dalpatram, he too said that I should deliver a lecture. On 27 May, I delivered a public lecture and thus met a lot of my old acquaintances who had come to attend.

24. On arriving in Surat, I delivered another lecture in the Andrews Library on 31 May and then left for Bombay.

25. In that year, I published *Narmakavita*, first in instalments and finally, as an entire book. This was my third book.

26. In September, I started the newsletter *Dandiyo* and also published the third volume of *Narmakosh*.

27. The expenses of my father's customary death rituals,
a drop in the sales of books (largely because the share
frenzy diverted the attention of the people away from
reading), my high household expenses (the rent for my
house in Bombay was Rs 75) and my spendthrift nature
all led to my financial condition weighing heavily
on my mind. I had run up a debt of about Rs 6,000.
This also made me adopt a perverse, contrarian stance
towards controlling my expenses, as if to challenge
providence, saying, 'Let us see how long these strained
circumstances will last!' I was further embittered that
no financial help was forthcoming from my wealthy
friends. To console myself, I spent money—largely on
helping those in need and to encourage artists I deemed
worthy. It angered me when I saw the nouveau riche
squandering their wealth on courtesans and singers
who had no understanding of music. In an effort to
help and encourage good singers, I arranged a concert
with about twenty-five singers on Aso Vad 10. At the
end of the concert, which lasted all through the night,
I rewarded each one of them suitably and spent Rs 200.

28. The Frayer Land Reclamation Company was formed
in November, and my friend Karsandas Madhavdas

was one of its promoters. He had offered shares of the company to many of his friends. Some of my friends advised me to go and meet him so that I too would be given shares. I declined, saying that if it occurred to him, well and good, I was not going to ask him. They quoted the Gujarati proverb to me: 'Even a mother does not serve unless asked.' I retorted, 'A mother will serve even her most stubborn son. A friend, if he wants to, will give without being asked.' Some criticized me for my naivety and labelled it pig-headedness; some even spoke ill of Karsandas. I deflected them with varying replies—to some I said I had already received shares, to some that I was about to receive them. To some I said that I was already under deep obligation to Karsandas and therefore it didn't matter if I wasn't given shares. One day, one of my Nagar friends said, 'Kavi, please don't miss this opportunity. I absolutely insist that you must approach Karsandas. Go for my sake, if not yours.' I capitulated to his sincere insistence and promised him that I would approach Karsandas. But by the time I reached my home, I had changed my mind.

It so happened that Karsandas invited me to his home on his birthday. I was to go with another friend of mine in his carriage. I was clear that I would not bring up any issue regarding shares. At nine that night, my friend called to cancel, citing ill health. He also said that the carriage would not be available. I, too, intended to cancel, considering that it was already late. But then it occurred to me that I would be leaving for Surat to conduct the death rituals for my father and it would be some time before I could return. It was perhaps best that I met Karsandas before leaving. I hired a carriage and went. Some friends were still there. Karandas sat me beside him as soon as I entered and whispered in my ear, 'I have reserved one share for you.' I said, 'That was hardly necessary!' I recited several poems that night, mostly ones of Vira Rasa, and they were much appreciated by those present. Balaji Pandurang, who had always admired my poems of valour, particularly appreciated my recitation of *Hinduoni Padti*, the Decline of the Hindus. After a few days, I sold the share that Karsandas had given and it fetched me a profit of Rs 5,700. I settled my debt in full and at the end of December, I arrived in Surat.

29. On arrival in Surat, one of my aunts passed away, and I had to postpone all the customary rituals of my

father's death by about fifteen days. In the interim, I decided to visit Dabhoi and collect some material on Dayaram. I got off at Miyagam with a plan to take a short route along the new road that the Gaikwad had constructed from Miyagam to Dabhoi. I hired a wagon and set off with three companions and the son of a grocer from Dabhoi as a guide. The road was in a bad shape, and the wagon could go no further than about 20 kilometres. We decided to walk the rest of the way. It was night, the terrain was uneven and the path was in very bad condition. Narbheram and I enjoyed the experience of fumbling our way there, surrounded by the sounds of the jungle. Braving the biting cold, tired and hungry, we walked 25 kilometres, finally reaching the gates of Dabhoi at 3 in the morning. The gates were shut for the night, and we had to spend the rest of the night in a wagon that was parked there. At dawn, we got the gates opened and went to a dharamshala near the lake, where we broke our fast. We were planning on renting a house for three days when we realized that Chanod–Karnali were only about 20 kilometres away. Both are places of pilgrimage on the banks of the Narmada and were likely to be scenic spots. We decided to visit them and immediately hired a bullock cart. We reached Chanod at about 1 in the afternoon. While passing through the town, we were set upon by the Brahmins, who plagued us with questions: what sort of Brahmins are you? Where are you from? Who is your family priest? And so on. We ignored them and made our way to the house of Narbheram's friend, where we planned to put up. We had some light refreshments and immediately left for Karnali, which was just about 3 kilometres away. We walked along the banks of the river. On the way, there is a confluence with the Orsang river, where we bathed. We roamed around, visited the temples and returned to Chanod by 5 p.m. We had our dinner and once again went out into the night to the temple of Sheshasayee, where we attended the evening arti. I was descending the stairs of the temple when a Brahmin, who was reciting his prayers, asked my companion, 'Is that Narmadashankar?' The companion ignored the query but when he persisted, another of my companions confirmed that I was indeed Narmadashankar. He called out to me and I recognized that he was Ranchhod, a disciple of Dayaram. I went up to talk with him and he said, 'I will reach Dabhoi the day after tomorrow. Please stay there till then.' I said that I had made the trip specifically to see him

and that he should definitely meet us in Dabhoi. We
roamed around in the night along the banks of the
Narmada before returning to our lodging place. We
slept at about 11, and at 5 the next morning, we left
for Dabhoi.

30. Chanod has a significant Brahmin population. They
depend on pilgrims for their livelihood. They are
greedy, sly and brash, but their women come across
as kind and affectionate. The women of Chanod–
Karnali are known for their licentious behaviour—
typical of a place of pilgrimage! The stories we had
heard were only confirmed by an experience we
had. One of my companions was approached by a
Brahmin woman who took him to her home. 'This
is our kitchen, this is where we sleep, this is my
daughter and this is my daughter-in-law; had you
put up with us, we could have taken good care of
you. Please stay with us the next time you visit.' The
tone clearly indicated that all the needs would be
taken care of. The women came across as genuinely
caring and concerned. Perhaps the greed for money
had instilled such habits in them from childhood.
There are no Nagars in Chanod.

31. Karnali is a smaller village than Chanod. It has a large population of Nagar Brahmins and Maharashtrians. The men pursue Vedic studies. The women are similar to those of Chanod but being Nagars, they are smarter and more enticing. I did not like Chanod at all, but Karnali is blessed with natural beauty and so it appealed to me. The landscape in the evening light was so beautiful that words fail me in trying to describe it. Vast open spaces dotted with small trees, undulating hills farther away in the distance and little stone temples scattered along the riverbank! Solitude, peace and tranquillity! Truly a place to spend the evening of one's life! It was the perfect place of pilgrimage. Most of the places of pilgrimage along the Narmada are quite scenic. The steps of the ghats at Karnali are tricky— one could easily slip if one was climbing them in haste. Once, while sitting on the steps of the Somnath temple after the darshan, a thought occurred to me: to be in the midst of such solemn and tranquil beauty in the latter part of one's life would give such joy—a joy that stemmed from the contentment of having lived a meaningful life. It is indeed gratifying to cherish in one's waning years the sweet memories of fruitful labour and meaningful relationships of one's youth.

Would I, in the autumn of my life, after completing my sojourn, be able to find the time and place to sit like this, with a joyful heart, and experience oneness with the Infinite?

The idea of social reform has not touched those villages (Chanod and Karnali).[*] Despite its widespread influence, reform seems to have given these villages a miss. While returning to Dabhoi, I felt sorry for the inhabitants of Chanod and Karnali. Would they ever be redeemed? The social reformers of Bombay are paying mere lip service. I thought of writing an essay proposing the need to establish a mission for social reform. Those involved in the mission would travel to remote places and spread the word of reform there. Some reformers think reform is restricted to rules of eating and wearing clothes; they are ashamed of sitting with the poor and the ignorant. They do not go out into the remote districts. What use, then, are their sermons?

32. Having left Chanod in the morning, we arrived in Dabhoi at about 11 a.m. We booked a room in a dharamshala. On the one hand, we made preparations

---

[*] On reaching Bombay, I sent a few booklets that I had compiled, costing Rs 50, to some of the inhabitants of Karnali as gifts.

for cooking, while on the other, we set out to conduct our research on Dayaram. In Bombay, at the home of Bhai Chimanlal, I had met a Mathur Kayastha by the name of Naranmal Harakhmal, a resident of Dabhoi. He had said to me, 'If you come to Dabhoi, I can get you access to Dayaram's books from Ghelabhai Dulabhdas Jamindar.' We looked for Ghelabhai, but he wasn't in Dabhoi then, having gone to his native village. One of his relatives came to meet us, and we talked about Dayaram. He informed us that Ghelabhai would be arriving that evening. After lunch, we ventured out into the town in search of Dayaram's house. The people, on hearing our query about where Dayaram lived, were astonished that we were concerned about someone who was long dead and gone! Finally, we did manage to locate the house, about which references can be found in Dayaram's biography. The next morning, we tried to meet Ghelabhai, but the family members, thinking we were officers from the state administration, said that he wasn't home. I decided to go in person, hoping to explain, but was turned away from the door with the story that he wasn't home, although I knew that he was. Such was the fear of the Gaikwad's state and the condition of the state's citizens! We made more inquiries regarding Dayaram in the town, but not finding any books or documents, we thought of leaving Dabhoi. However, since Ranchhod had promised that he would be arriving in Dabhoi, we decided to stay for two days more and see a bit more of the town.

Dabhoi has four gates—one leading to Vadodara, one to Champaner, one to Nandod state and the fourth is the Heera Gate. The name Heera Gate has an interesting story behind it. Heera was a mason who fell in love with Taina, one of the king's slaves. Heera had promised his beloved that he would immortalize her name. Stones were being brought from Marwad to construct the lake in Dabhoi. Heera stole some stones from here to construct another lake, a few miles away, where his beloved lived. It is even today known as Tain Lake. It is largish in size and despite its age, not a stone seems to have been damaged. The water is milky white and sweet. When the king heard of the construction of Tain Lake, he decided to punish Heera by immuring him in the very gate whose arch he was constructing. Heera's aides, however, managed to keep a small hole in the wall behind which Heera was confined. They managed to pour ghee into the hole, which went straight into Heera's mouth and kept him alive. No other mason could manage to complete the arch of the gate, and the king released Heera to allow him to complete the arch, after which he was imprisoned again. Hence the name Heera Gate. Just touching the gate is a small temple of Goddess Kali. The stonework is quite impressive. We saw the hole from which the ghee was said to have been poured, but dismissed the story as mere legend. There is some engraving in Sanskrit on the stones, but, being badly worn, it is indecipherable. The town has a large population of Brahmins and Kanbis. There are many Sathodara Nagars here. It is one of the administrative centres of the Gaikwad's state. There is a palace dating back to the times of the Peshwa by the lake.

33. Ranchhod did not keep his promise of coming to Dabhoi from Chanod, and I couldn't lay my hands on books by Dayaram. I was very disappointed and hired a bullock cart to leave for Vadodara right away. The plan was to take a train to Surat, but since one wasn't available immediately, I decided to go to Ahmedabad instead. The reason was that since November, I had been planning to create a library of Gujarati books in my home. I wanted to procure books for that library from Ahmedabad. On reaching Ahmedabad,

I immediately went to the library there and asked them for their catalogue of Gujarati books. I was told that there were very few Gujarati books, and although there was a catalogue, it wasn't immediately locatable. They would look for it the next day. I asked if they had any manuscripts. They replied in the negative but said that there might be some at the Vernacular Society. I then went to Mahipatram's home, where I would be staying. I did not see any good collection of Gujarati books in Ahmedabad. At the insistence of Jagjivandas Deputy, I delivered a lecture at his home. He had made considerable effort and invited all the Sethias. I also received news that a handwritten manuscript written by Samal was available with the descendants of one of his students. I requested Mahipatram to somehow procure that manuscript and send it to me. I then left for Surat.

34. After completing the customary death rites of my father, I left for Takarma village near Olpad, where a poet named Nabhulal lived. I reached by nightfall. Nabhulal was employed as a talati. He was at that time composing Gujarati poetry based on the Vedant. In the past, he had composed several lyrical poems on Radha–

Krishna. Although not an advocate of any particular religious ideology, Nabhulal had managed to draw many followers wherever he lived. The weavers of Surat were his disciples. Five years ago, when I saw him in Surat, his disciples would perform arti as a mark of their devotion to him. Although a man of poetic sensibility, he is quite social and understands the ways of the world. His poetry, although not of the highest quality, was stylistically faithful to the traditional norms of poetics. His disciples asked me to recite my poems. Assuming that their inclination lay towards Vedantic thought, I recited my poem 'Anubhav Laheri'. I then said, 'Many Vedantis focus on the symbolic significance of words and their underlying meanings. Based on this understanding, they consider themselves to have understood the idea of "Aham Brahmasmi", or "I am the Brahman". This is not meant to be taken literally. What this essentially means is that it is only the individual who understands the divine play of the inner and the outer world and derives everlasting joy from this realization can really say that he is the Brahman, or "Aham Brahmasmi".'

The following morning, we gathered again in Nabhulal's courtyard and carried on the discussion while sipping our tea. Once again, his disciples asked me Vedant-related questions. I said to them quite clearly, 'I have not studied Vedantic texts. I am only a poet. If you have questions about poetics, feel free to ask.' The matter ended there. Meanwhile, Nabhulal recited some of his old and new poems and read out mine. Once everyone left, Nabhulal and I sat down to read Vedantic texts. I asked Nabhulal, 'What is the difference between you and me?' He said, 'Not much. You also exemplify the notion of Aham Brahmasmi. But I would suggest that you engage in a deeper study of the texts.' Once, I had asked Vishnubawa Brahmachari of Bombay, 'I request you to teach me Vedant.' He was also of the view, 'You have already understood the essence of Vedant.' We then had lunch. At night, we sat once again. I asked him a few questions to observe his method of conducting a debate. I realized that he did not draw from argument, but rather focused on illustrations when he debated. Nabhulal has always had affection for me. The next day, I left Takarma and arrived in Surat.

Viram 10

1865–66

1. I went to Bombay in January.

2. I have, for many years, harboured a strong desire to travel to north India. My desire to travel through India is stronger than my desire to travel to England. It does not feel right to travel to England before having seen India properly. Besides, unlike many of my acquaintances, I am not interested in experiencing England's pomp and glory. My motivation is to see England's natural beauty, observe the ways of its people and interact with its intellectuals. Actually, that is also my motivation to travel within India. When Dr Bhau, Ardeshar Faramji Moos, Khorsedji Nasarwanji Cama, Rustomji Khorsedji Cama et al. planned their sojourn across India, I had expressed my desire to join them (to

Dr Bhau and Ardeshar Faramji). They were both happy to have me accompany them, but I did not have the resources to meet my expenses then. Dr Bhau offered to defray part of my expenses but expressed his concern that Khorsedji Cama would be hesitant to bear any additional expense. Ardeshar also advised me that in such matters, it was inappropriate to burden someone else. I, too, felt that there was no dignity in relying on others. Also, I did not want to make haste during such a trip; it would defeat the very purpose. I dropped the idea then, telling myself that I would travel sometime in the future when I had money of my own, rather than relying on the charity of my wealthy friends.

3.   Sometime last year, I had brought up the subject with my friend Karsandas Madhavdas, saying, 'I wish to travel across Hindustan. If between you and some of your merchant friends, you could make a provision of about 10,000 rupees, I would be able to prepare two comprehensive volumes of prose and poetry, which would defray the cost of my travels.' He had agreed. I thought that the merchants were flush with earnings from the share market, and this would not be a particularly heavy burden. In any case, if this did

not work out, I could delay my travels by a few more years. Having experienced Karsandas's affection for me since 1855 and having observed the pride he took in my achievements, I was confident that he would stand by me in my time of need. I do not quite remember the year, but when Kavi Dalpatram had approached Bombay's wealthy patrons to build his home in Ahmedabad, he had presented Karsandas with a picture-poem singing his praises and had followed up with the prayer that he be rewarded with Rs 5,000. Karsandas had not responded. Karsandas himself had narrated the incident to me, adding, 'Kavi Dalpatram's way for asking for help was completely inappropriate. What is my relationship with him? Why shouldn't I give to my Narmad instead?'

A few months later, my friend sent me a cheque of Rs 5,000.

4. Having apprised Karsandas of my plans to publish, I gave my collection of prose to Ganpat Krishnaji in March and my collection of poetry to Union Press in June for printing. The prose collection was published in September of the same year. As for the collection of poetry, it is now September 1866, but it hasn't seen the light of day.

5. That year, the share market saw a downturn, and the sales of my books dropped. I had stopped my teaching for the past two years. The constant visits of my friends and acquaintances were a disturbance that affected my creative output. Since I was still hoping to make my travel plans a reality, I had already made arrangements for my wife to stay in Surat. Now, to reduce my expenses, I decided to shift base to Surat myself in July 1865. Although I would be staying mainly in Surat, I would have to come to Bombay for my work and for that, I have also rented a home in Bombay.

6. My publications in that year were the collection of prose mentioned earlier, *Narmakavya* Vol. 1, and the second edition of a collection of Dayaram's poetry.[*] During that year and ever since, I haven't written much poetry. Most of my time was spent in correcting the proofs and providing the material to the press.

7. On 10 September, a Sunday morning, I was taken by my friends Girdharlal Dayaldas and Nagindas

---

[*] I had sent two of my students to Vadodara and Dabhoi to collect some poems and a picture of Dayaram (the one obtained previously was not correct).

Tulsidas to meet Sir Alexander Grant. On being introduced by my friends, he received me with great respect. Mr Oxenham, a professor of literature, and Mr Buhler, a professor of Sanskrit, were also present. Mr Grant was greatly pleased when I showed him my books and urged me to recite from them. I explained, 'Unlike English poetry, our Prakrit poetry is not recited plainly but is sung. I am hesitant to sing since I fear that my Gujarati singing may not be pleasing to your ears.' He said, 'I realize that, but do sing nevertheless.' When I inquired if he would like to listen to a romantic poem or one of valour, he said, 'Romantic poetry, unquestionably.' I then sang the lavani 'Sha Hata Aapna Bahar' (How Wonderful Was Our Spring), and as I ended, he exclaimed, 'What a beautiful recitation!' When I explained the meaning, all three were quite pleased. Girdharlal and Nagindas explained the meaning of 'Vaadal Faatva Mandyun' (The Cloud Burst) and 'Utho Dhari Umang' (O, Rise in Joy). I also sang and explained the verses on the monsoon, written in Mandakranta and Harini *chhand*, from my *Rituvarnan*. I then told them I was in need of financial help to publish my books as well as to travel across Hindustan. He

said, 'Do make an application.* I will see that you
get substantial help.' When we were about to leave,
he said, 'Please provide me with a translation** of
that lavani into English. I will send it to my friend,
the Poet Laureate Tennyson.' Thus, having spent
about an hour and a half with them, we shook hands
and parted.

8. In January 1866, I purchased the land opposite my
house for Rs 600 and began the construction of a
new house. I also commissioned the repairs of my old
home. With regard to the construction of my new
house, I had, on several occasions, had differences
with Mr Summers, the deputy collector. The news
went around town that the Kavi was shifting to Surat

---

* Based on my application, it was decided that my books should be sent
to Raosaheb Mahipatram for examination. I sent the books to him, and
he reviewed them too. I am sorry to say that whereas I had expected
a minimum of Rs. 2,000, Grant has written to sanction an amount of
Rs. 600.

** I translated the lavani into English and sent it to a few of my college
friends as well as some Englishmen who suggested some modifications.
However, I feel that the translation does not have the impact of the
original Gujarati and therefore, I haven't sent it yet.

and the hat-wearers were fighting his move. From the time I stood up to him, Mr Summers, who had hitherto wreaked terror on the residents, cooled down somewhat. Later, he became completely tame after questions about him were raised in the government itself (both homes were ready by September).

9. I published *Suratni Mukhtesar Hakikat* in April, *Narma Vyakarana* Vol. 2, Part I, in June and *Narmakosh* Vol. 4 in September of that year.

10. On 9 August, I received news in Surat of the sad death of my dear friend Raobahadur Ramchandra Balkrishna, who had passed away on 2 August. I was deeply perturbed at the sudden passing of Ramchandra, whom we all addressed as Bhai. Although our meetings were infrequent, whenever we met, it was like old friends and fellow travellers on the path of nation building. I was reminded of how we spent many an hour discussing issues of social and religious reform. Even at community gatherings, leaving the other members present there, the two of us would retire to a quiet corner where we could talk in peace. Matters of social reform were always the focus of our conversations, even

when we met at our homes. I was reminded of how he had once told me that since I was making the Mission House in Surat, I should invite him to Surat. I was also reminded of our train journey together to Bombay. These sweet memories flooded my mind on hearing of his unexpected passing and greatly saddened me. He firmly believed that in matters of social reform, one should pursue an aggressive stance for reform. I, on the other hand, believed that a mission for social reform should be formed, and gradually, once the number of members increased, we could push aggressively for reform (considering the present circumstances, the formation of such a mission is unlikely, and so I have come to believe that those who can afford to and wish to, can aggressively push for reform, endure the pain involved and console themselves that, at the very least, they would be remembered for their courage). Bhai had a softer corner for me than for other Gujarati social reformers. I have rarely seen a person who, like him, was endowed with the virtues of simplicity, humility, punctiliousness, independence, affection and courage. And as far as love for and loyalty to friends go, he had few equals!

11. On 9 August, I had many differences with my caste/ community, and I should write about it. But since I intend to take up many more issues on the differences that I have with them, perhaps I should write about it at length on a later occasion.

12. On 31 August, Kavi Nabhulal Danatram visited me. I asked him, 'What, according to you, is a mark of great poetry?' To which he replied, 'Poetry that allows multiple meanings.' I further asked, 'Let us say one person captures accurately the underlying meaning but the language employed is turgid, and another person uses language that is lucid but does not capture the meaning well. Which of the two would you rank higher?' His answer was, 'The lucid one.' He explained further, 'Poetry without meaning is lifeless, whereas poetry which is turgid is weak poetry.' 'Very well,' I said. 'Which is better—something that is weak but alive or a thing of beauty that is lifeless?' He replied, 'What is alive, of course.'

13. On the night of 3 September, Bhai Mansukhram Surajram and Ranchhodbhai Uderam visited me in

Bombay. I expressed to them my thoughts on reform, which are somewhat as follows:

> My goal is to ensure that people, on their own, with unfettered minds, apply reason and justice to practices and, once they derive their own set of principles, apply them to all future actions.
>
> If in this course, while applying an unfettered mind and implementing the principles so derived, the leaders among them cross certain boundaries, it may appear that they are actually working against reform. I would not, in such circumstances, say that they have caused damage to society. During monsoon, there is darkness and there are storms. However, in the season that follows, one sees the green fields that act as a salve for the eyes.
>
> The Hindus are bound by the twin nooses of religion and social obligations. So tight are the coils of these nooses that unless a few brave persons make desperate attempts to cut these bonds, take radical steps to bring about change (even if they be accused of impropriety), true reform cannot occur. There is no place for incremental reform among the Hindus—it

has to be radical. For some time, perhaps, the results may be undesirable, but what of it?

It is a time of war—a war between superstition and reform. It is not a time to teach ethics. The rules of war are different; one needs to use all the means available—persuasion, enticement, threat and intrigue. New kingdoms often arise from the ravages of a revolution.

14. This year, my mind has been seized with two concerns: love and money. However, I have tried to conquer these feelings by taking refuge in the path of knowledge. As for the former, I seem to have come out of it. In August and September, I suffered from a venereal disease. I even wrote a short piece, 'Nayikapravesh', to make light of the matter. My trust was betrayed by three members of my family and some friends. This has upset me deeply.

15. The above is the truthful narrative of the thirty-three years of my life so far. Many of the events can be located in the various issues of *Budhhivardhak Granth*, *Satyadeepak*, *Rast Goftar*, *Samsherbahadur* etc.

16. There are many thoughts and actions concerning my romantic relationships, my finances, religion and reform that, if written about now, would cause damage to my relations with several persons and cause undesirable reactions among ordinary people, whose ability to understand them is limited. I think it prudent to present those at a more opportune time in the future. For the present, this is enough.

Surat, 18 September 1866
Bhadarva Sud 9, Samvat 1922

Scan QR code to access the
Penguin Random House India website